THIS BOOK BELONGS TO

The Library of

....

....

I can't tell you how grateful I am that you decided to read my book. My most heartfelt thanks that you took time out of your life to choose my work and I hope you find benefit within these pages.

There are so many books available today that offer similar content so that makes it even more humbling that you decided to buying mine.

Tell me what you thought! I am eager to hear your opinion and ideas on what you read as are others who are looking for a good book to buy. Leave a review on Amazon.com so others can benefit from your wisdom!

With much thanks.

Table of Contents

SUMMARY

Irish crochet is a unique form of lace-making that originated in Ireland during the mid-19th century. It is characterized by its intricate designs, delicate motifs, and the use of a variety of stitches and techniques. The art of Irish crochet was developed as a response to the devastating potato famine that plagued Ireland during that time.

During the famine, many Irish families were forced to leave their homes and seek refuge in other countries. As they traveled, they brought with them their traditional skills in lace-making, which they adapted and evolved to suit their new surroundings. This led to the emergence of Irish crochet as a distinct style of lace-making.

Irish crochet lace is known for its three-dimensional quality, achieved through the use of padded and raised stitches. This technique gives the lace a unique texture and depth, making it stand out from other forms of lace-making. The motifs used in Irish crochet are often inspired by nature, with flowers, leaves, and vines being common themes.

The popularity of Irish crochet grew rapidly during the late 19th and early 20th centuries. It became a significant cottage industry in Ireland, providing employment for many women who were skilled in the craft. Irish crochet lace was highly sought after, both domestically and internationally, and was often used to adorn clothing, accessories, and household items.

However, the art of Irish crochet faced a decline in the mid-20th century due to changing fashion trends and the rise of machine-made lace. The traditional techniques and intricate designs of Irish crochet were gradually forgotten, and the craft became less popular.

In recent years, there has been a resurgence of interest in Irish crochet. Crafters and lace enthusiasts have rediscovered the beauty and intricacy of this traditional lace-making technique. There are now dedicated groups and organizations that promote and preserve the art of Irish crochet, ensuring that this unique form of lace-making continues to thrive.

Today, Irish crochet is celebrated for its rich history and cultural significance. It is considered a valuable part of Ireland's heritage and is often showcased in museums and exhibitions. The intricate designs and delicate motifs of Irish crochet continue to inspire and captivate lace-makers and crafters around the world.

In recent years, there has been a notable resurgence of interest in the art of Irish crochet. This traditional craft, which originated in Ireland in the 19th century, involves creating intricate lace-like designs using a combination of crochet stitches and motifs. While Irish crochet had experienced a decline in popularity over the years, it is now experiencing a revival as more and more people are discovering its beauty and versatility.

One of the reasons for the renewed interest in Irish crochet is its unique and distinctive aesthetic. The delicate and intricate designs created through this technique are truly breathtaking. From delicate flowers and leaves to intricate geometric patterns, Irish crochet allows for endless possibilities in design. The use of fine thread and small crochet hooks adds to the intricacy of the finished pieces, making them truly works of art.

Another factor contributing to the resurgence of Irish crochet is the growing interest in traditional crafts and handmade items. In a world dominated by mass-produced goods, there is a growing desire for unique and one-of-a-kind items. Irish crochet, with its rich history and intricate craftsmanship, offers a way for individuals to create something truly special and meaningful. The process of creating Irish crochet pieces requires time, patience, and skill, making the end result all the more valuable.

Furthermore, the accessibility of resources and information has played a significant role in the revival of Irish crochet. With the advent of the internet, enthusiasts can easily access patterns, tutorials, and forums dedicated to Irish crochet. This has allowed for the sharing of knowledge and techniques, making it easier for beginners to learn and master this intricate craft. Additionally, the availability of high-quality crochet threads and hooks has made it easier for individuals to obtain the necessary materials to create their own Irish crochet masterpieces.

The resurgence of interest in Irish crochet has also been fueled by the desire to preserve and celebrate cultural heritage. Irish crochet has a rich history deeply rooted in Irish culture and tradition. By reviving this craft, individuals are not only creating beautiful pieces of art but also paying homage to their Irish heritage. This sense of connection to one's roots has resonated with many, leading to a renewed appreciation for Irish crochet.

In conclusion, the resurgence of interest in Irish crochet can be attributed to its unique aesthetic, the growing interest in traditional crafts, the accessibility of resources, and the desire to preserve cultural heritage. As more and more people discover the beauty and versatility of this craft, Irish crochet is once again taking its rightful place as a cherished art form.

A. Materials and tools

The input for this task is the list of materials and tools required to complete a specific project or task. This could include a wide range of items, depending on the nature of the project.

Materials refer to the physical substances or components that are needed to carry out the task. This could include things like wood, metal, plastic, fabric, paint, screws, nails, glue, or any other material that is necessary for the project. The specific materials required will depend on the nature of the project and the desired outcome. For example, if the task is to build a wooden bookshelf, the materials required would include wooden boards, screws, and possibly paint or varnish for finishing.

Tools, on the other hand, are the instruments or devices that are used to manipulate or work with the materials. This could include hand tools such as hammers, screwdrivers, wrenches, or pliers, as well as power tools like drills, saws, or sanders. The specific tools required will depend on the complexity of the project and the specific tasks that need to be performed. For example, if the task is to assemble a piece of furniture, the tools required would include a screwdriver, a hammer, and possibly a drill.

It is important to have a comprehensive and accurate list of materials and tools before starting a project. This ensures that all necessary items are available and minimizes the risk of delays or interruptions during the project. It is also important to consider the quality and suitability of the materials and tools chosen. Using high-quality materials and tools can result in a better end product and a more efficient and enjoyable working process.

In conclusion, the input for this task is the list of materials and tools required to complete a project or task. This includes the physical substances or components needed (materials) as well as the instruments or devices used to manipulate them (tools). Having a comprehensive and accurate list of materials and tools is essential for a successful and efficient project.

Traditional Irish motifs are a rich and vibrant part of Irish culture and art. These motifs are deeply rooted in the country's history and have been passed down through generations. They are often seen in various forms of art, including textiles, pottery, and jewelry.

One of the most iconic traditional Irish motifs is the Celtic knot. These intricate and interwoven designs are characterized by their continuous lines and loops, symbolizing the eternal cycle of life and nature. Celtic knots can be found in various forms, such as the Trinity knot, which represents the Holy Trinity in Christianity, and the Lover's knot, symbolizing eternal love and unity.

Another popular motif in Irish art is the shamrock. This three-leafed clover is widely recognized as a symbol of Ireland and is associated with St. Patrick, the patron saint of the country. The shamrock is believed to have been used by St. Patrick to explain the concept of the Holy Trinity to the Irish people. Today, it is often used as a symbol of good luck and is commonly seen in jewelry, clothing, and decorations.

The Claddagh ring is another traditional Irish motif that holds great significance. This distinctive ring features a heart, a crown, and two hands, symbolizing love, loyalty, and friendship. The heart represents love, the crown represents loyalty, and the hands represent friendship. The Claddagh ring is often given as a token of love or friendship and is passed down through generations as a cherished heirloom.

Irish crosses are also prominent motifs in traditional Irish art. These crosses are often adorned with intricate Celtic knotwork and are associated with Christianity. The Celtic cross, with its distinctive circle intersecting the cross, is a powerful symbol of faith and heritage. It is commonly seen in graveyards, churches, and as decorative elements in Irish homes.

In addition to these motifs, traditional Irish art often incorporates symbols of nature, such as animals, plants, and landscapes. Animals like the stag, the hare, and the salmon are frequently depicted in Irish art, representing strength, fertility, and wisdom. Plants like the oak tree and the shamrock are also commonly used, symbolizing endurance and good fortune. Landscapes, particularly those featuring rolling hills, rugged coastlines, and ancient ruins, are often depicted in paintings and tapestries, capturing the beauty and mystique of the Irish countryside.

Contemporary Irish crochet designs are a beautiful and intricate form of crochet that originated in Ireland. This style of crochet is known for its delicate and lacy appearance, created by using fine thread and intricate stitch patterns.

Irish crochet designs have a rich history, dating back to the 19th century when they were used to create stunning lace garments and accessories. However, contemporary Irish crochet designs have evolved to incorporate modern elements and techniques, making them even more unique and eye-catching.

One of the defining features of contemporary Irish crochet designs is the use of motifs. These motifs can be anything from flowers and leaves to geometric shapes and intricate patterns. They are typically worked separately and then joined together to create a larger piece, such as a shawl or a tablecloth. The motifs are often embellished with additional stitches and techniques, such as picots and bullion stitches, to add texture and depth to the design.

Another characteristic of contemporary Irish crochet designs is the use of different types of stitches. While traditional Irish crochet primarily uses basic crochet stitches, such as single crochet and double crochet, contemporary designs often incorporate more complex stitches, such as popcorn stitches and cluster stitches. These stitches create interesting textures and patterns, adding a modern twist to the traditional technique.

Contemporary Irish crochet designs also often incorporate other elements, such as beads, sequins, and embroidery. These embellishments can be added to the motifs or used to create additional details and accents. They add a touch of glamour and sophistication to the designs, making them perfect for special occasions or formal events.

In addition to garments and accessories, contemporary Irish crochet designs can also be used to create home decor items, such as doilies, curtains, and pillow covers. These pieces add a touch of elegance and charm to any space, and can be customized to match any decor style.

Overall, contemporary Irish crochet designs are a stunning and versatile form of crochet that combines traditional techniques with modern elements. Whether you're a seasoned crocheter or a beginner, exploring this style of crochet can be a rewarding and enjoyable experience. So why not give it a try and create your own beautiful and unique Irish crochet masterpiece?

Advanced Irish crochet techniques refer to the intricate and complex methods used in creating exquisite and highly detailed crochet designs. Irish crochet itself is a traditional form of crochet that originated in Ireland in the 19th century. It is characterized by its use of motifs, lace-like patterns, and three-dimensional elements.

To delve into advanced Irish crochet techniques, one must first have a solid foundation in basic crochet stitches and techniques. These include chain stitches, slip stitches, single crochet, double crochet, and treble crochet. Once these fundamentals are mastered, crocheters can then progress to more advanced techniques.

One of the key aspects of advanced Irish crochet is the creation of motifs. These motifs are typically small, intricate designs that are joined together to form larger pieces such as shawls, doilies, or even garments. The motifs can be inspired by nature, such as flowers, leaves, or butterflies, or they can be abstract designs. Creating these motifs requires a high level of precision and attention to detail.

Another important technique in advanced Irish crochet is the use of lace-like patterns. These patterns are created by combining various stitches and techniques to form delicate and openwork designs. Common stitches used in lace patterns include picots, clusters, and shells. Crocheters must have a good understanding of stitch placement and tension to achieve the desired lace effect.

Three-dimensional elements are also a hallmark of advanced Irish crochet. These elements, such as flowers or leaves, are created separately and then attached to the main piece. They add depth and texture to the crochet work, making it more visually appealing. Creating these three-dimensional elements requires shaping techniques, such as increasing and decreasing stitches, as well as careful assembly.

In addition to these techniques, advanced Irish crochet often incorporates other decorative elements, such as beading or embroidery. Beads can be added to the crochet work to create a sparkling effect, while embroidery can be used to add intricate details or embellishments.

Mastering advanced Irish crochet techniques requires patience, practice, and a keen eye for detail. It is a labor-intensive craft that rewards those who are willing to invest the time and effort. The end result is a stunning piece of crochet work that showcases the beauty and intricacy of this traditional craft.

A comprehensive collection of meticulously crafted step-by-step patterns for a wide range of Irish crochet projects, designed to cater to the diverse interests and skill levels of crochet enthusiasts. This invaluable resource offers an extensive array of detailed instructions, accompanied by visually appealing illustrations, to guide you through the intricate process of creating stunning Irish crochet masterpieces.

Whether you are a beginner looking to embark on your first Irish crochet project or an experienced crocheter seeking new challenges, this compilation has something for everyone. From delicate lace doilies and elegant table runners to intricate shawls and exquisite garments, the patterns cover a vast spectrum of items that can be adorned with the timeless beauty of Irish crochet.

Each pattern is thoughtfully crafted to ensure clarity and ease of understanding, making it accessible even to those who are new to the art of Irish crochet. The step-by-step instructions take you through every stage of the project, from selecting the appropriate yarn and hook size to mastering the intricate stitches and techniques that define Irish crochet. With detailed explanations and helpful tips, you will gain a deep understanding of the unique characteristics and nuances of this traditional craft.

The patterns are organized in a logical and user-friendly manner, allowing you to easily navigate through the book and find the project that captures your interest. Each pattern is accompanied by a list of materials required, ensuring that you have everything you need before you begin. Additionally, the book provides guidance on choosing suitable color combinations and embellishments, enabling you to personalize your creations and add your own artistic touch.

The visual appeal of the book is enhanced by the inclusion of high-quality photographs showcasing the finished projects in all their glory. These images serve as a source of inspiration, allowing you to envision the potential of each pattern and motivating you to embark on your own creative journey.

In addition to the patterns, the book also offers valuable insights into the history and cultural significance of Irish crochet. You will learn about the origins of this intricate craft, its evolution over the years, and the role it has played in Irish heritage. This contextual information adds depth and meaning to your crochet experience, allowing you to appreciate the rich tradition behind each stitch.

Whether you are seeking to expand your crochet skills, create unique and beautiful gifts, or simply indulge in the meditative and therapeutic nature of crochet, this collection of step-by-step patterns for various Irish crochet projects is an indispensable addition to your crafting library.

The output of showcasing the work of contemporary Irish crochet artists would involve a comprehensive and in-depth exploration of the intricate and captivating creations produced by these talented individuals. Irish crochet, a traditional craft that originated in Ireland in the 19th century, has evolved over time to incorporate modern techniques and designs, resulting in a vibrant and diverse range of artistic expressions.

The output would involve curating a visually stunning exhibition or publication that highlights the unique styles, techniques, and inspirations of contemporary Irish crochet artists. This would include showcasing a wide variety of crochet pieces, such as garments, accessories, home decor items, and even sculptural works, all created using the traditional Irish crochet techniques.

The output would also involve providing detailed information about each artist, their background, and their artistic journey. This would help to contextualize their work and provide a deeper understanding of their creative process. Additionally, it would be important to include interviews or statements from the artists themselves, allowing them to share their thoughts, inspirations, and motivations behind their creations.

Furthermore, the output would aim to educate and engage the audience by providing insights into the history and significance of Irish crochet as a craft. This could involve including historical references, archival materials, and explanations of the traditional techniques used in Irish crochet. By doing so, the output would not only showcase the contemporary work of Irish crochet artists but also pay homage to the rich heritage and cultural significance of this craft.

In order to create a more immersive experience, the output could also incorporate interactive elements. This could include workshops or demonstrations where visitors can learn basic Irish crochet techniques or even try their hand at creating their own small crochet piece. By actively involving the audience, the output would foster a deeper appreciation for the skill and artistry involved in Irish crochet.

Overall, the output of showcasing the work of contemporary Irish crochet artists would be a comprehensive and immersive experience that celebrates the beauty, innovation, and cultural significance of this traditional craft. It would provide a platform for these talented artists to gain recognition and appreciation for their work, while also educating and inspiring a wider audience about the art of Irish crochet.

Blocking and shaping are two essential techniques used in various fields, such as theater, dance, and visual arts, to create a visually appealing and impactful presentation or performance. These techniques involve the deliberate arrangement and positioning of elements, whether they are actors, objects, or movements, to effectively convey a message or tell a story.

In theater, blocking refers to the precise movement and positioning of actors on stage. It involves determining where actors should stand, walk, or interact with each other and the set. The purpose of blocking is to ensure that the actors' movements are coordinated and visually pleasing, while also enhancing the overall storytelling. By carefully blocking a scene, the director can guide the audience's attention to specific actions or dialogue, creating a more engaging and immersive experience.

Shaping, on the other hand, is the process of arranging and organizing the elements within a performance or artwork to create a desired composition or visual impact. This technique is commonly used in dance and visual arts, where the arrangement of dancers or objects can create a specific shape or pattern. Shaping allows artists to create visually striking images or movements that evoke certain emotions or convey a particular message.

Both blocking and shaping require careful consideration of various factors, such as the intended message, the space available, and the desired impact on the audience. They involve making deliberate choices about the placement, timing, and movement of elements to create a cohesive and visually appealing presentation.

In theater, blocking and shaping can greatly enhance the storytelling and emotional impact of a performance. By strategically positioning actors and objects on stage, directors can create dynamic and visually captivating scenes that effectively convey the intended message or evoke specific emotions. For example, a director may use blocking and shaping to create a sense of tension or intimacy between characters, or to highlight a particular moment of significance in the story.

In dance, blocking and shaping play a crucial role in creating visually stunning and expressive movements. Choreographers carefully arrange dancers on stage, considering their positions, formations, and interactions, to create captivating shapes and patterns. By using blocking and shaping techniques, dancers can effectively communicate their emotions and intentions to the audience, making the performance more engaging and memorable.

In visual arts, blocking and shaping are fundamental principles used to create visually appealing compositions. Artists carefully arrange objects, colors, and lines within a painting or sculpture to create a balanced and harmonious composition.

A comprehensive and extensive compilation of highly recommended books and online resources that cover a wide range of topics and interests. This compilation is designed to cater to various reading preferences and learning styles, ensuring that there is something for everyone.

The recommended books encompass a diverse selection of genres, including fiction, non-fiction, self-help, biographies, history, science, and more. Each book has been carefully chosen based on its quality, relevance, and impact, providing readers with an enriching and thought-provoking reading experience. Whether you are looking for a gripping novel to escape into a different world, a self-help book to enhance personal growth, or a historical account to deepen your understanding of the past, this list has got you covered.

In addition to the recommended books, the online resources included in this compilation offer a wealth of knowledge and information on various subjects. These resources range from educational websites, online courses, podcasts, TED Talks, and academic journals, among others. They provide a convenient and accessible way to expand your knowledge, learn new skills, and stay updated on the latest developments in your areas of interest.

The compilation of recommended books and online resources is not only suitable for avid readers and lifelong learners but also for students, professionals, and individuals seeking personal and professional development. Whether you are a student looking for additional resources to supplement your studies, a professional seeking to enhance your skills and knowledge in your field, or simply someone who enjoys learning and exploring new ideas, this compilation is a valuable tool to have at your disposal.

Furthermore, this compilation is regularly updated to ensure that it remains relevant and up-to-date with the latest releases and emerging online resources. It is a curated collection that has been meticulously researched and reviewed, saving you time and effort in finding high-quality books and online resources on your own.

Overall, the output of this compilation is a comprehensive and diverse collection of recommended books and online resources that cater to a wide range of interests and learning needs. It serves as a valuable guide for individuals seeking to expand their knowledge, explore new ideas, and engage in lifelong learning.

As I sit here and reflect on the journey of discovering Irish crochet, I am filled with a sense of awe and wonder. It all began with a simple curiosity, a desire to learn more about the rich history and intricate techniques of this traditional craft.

I remember stumbling upon a photograph of a stunning Irish crochet lace shawl, its delicate motifs and intricate patterns captivating my attention. I was immediately drawn to the beauty and complexity of the art form, and I knew I had to delve deeper into its origins and techniques.

My journey started with extensive research, diving into books, articles, and online resources to understand the history and evolution of Irish crochet. I discovered that it originated in Ireland during the famine years of the 19th century, when women used their creativity and resourcefulness to create intricate lace pieces as a means of income. This knowledge deepened my appreciation for the craft, as I realized the resilience and ingenuity of the women who pioneered this art form.

Armed with this newfound knowledge, I embarked on the practical aspect of my journey. I sought out experienced Irish crochet artisans, attending workshops and classes to learn the techniques and intricacies of the craft. It was a humbling experience to be surrounded by talented individuals who shared their expertise and passion for Irish crochet.

The process of creating my first Irish crochet piece was both challenging and rewarding. The intricate motifs and delicate stitches required patience and precision, but the end result was truly worth the effort. Holding the finished piece in my hands, I felt a deep sense of accomplishment and connection to the long line of artisans who came before me.

But my journey didn't end there. I soon realized that Irish crochet was not just a craft, but a community. I joined online forums and social media groups dedicated to Irish crochet, where I connected with fellow enthusiasts from around the world. We shared our projects, exchanged tips and techniques, and celebrated each other's successes. The sense of camaraderie and support within this community was truly inspiring, and it further fueled my passion for Irish crochet.

Reflecting on this journey, I am grateful for the opportunity to have discovered Irish crochet. It has not only enriched my life creatively, but it has also connected me to a vibrant and passionate community of artisans. The journey of discovering Irish crochet has been a transformative experience, one that has deepened my appreciation for the art form and the incredible individuals who continue to keep it alive.

My Wild Irish Rose Bedspread

MATERIALS: J. & P. COATS "KNIT-CRO-SHEEN" *or* BEDSPREAD COTTON: **Single Size Spread**—*72 x 108 inches (including fringe)*— *46 balls of White or Ecru, or 69 balls of any color,* **Double Size Spread**—*90 x 108 inches (including fringe)*—*58 balls of White or Ecru, or 87 balls of any color ... Steel Crochet Hook No. 7.*

GAUGE: Block measures 5 inches square.

FIRST BLOCK . . . Starting at center, ch 15. Join with sl st. **1st rnd:** Ch 1, 24 sc in ring. Sl st in 1st sc. **2nd rnd:** Ch 1, sc in same place as sl st, * ch 5, skip 2 sc, sc in next sc. Repeat from * around, ending with ch 5, sl st in 1st sc (8 loops). **3rd rnd:** In each loop around make sc, half dc, 5 dc, half dc and sc (8 petals). Sl st in 1st sc. **4th rnd:** * Ch 5, sc between next 2 petals. Repeat from * around. **5th rnd:** In each loop around make sc, half dc, 7 dc, half dc and sc. Sl st in 1st sc. **6th rnd:** Repeat 4th rnd, making ch 7 (instead of ch-5). **7th rnd:** Repeat 5th rnd, making 9 dc (instead of 7 dc). **8th rnd:** * Ch 5, in center st of petal make dc, ch 5 and dc; ch 5, sc between petals, ch 4, sl st in 3rd ch from hook (picot made), ch 2, picot, ch 1, sc in center st of next petal, ch 1, picot, ch 2, picot, ch 1, sc between petals. Repeat from * around. **9th rnd:** Sl st in next 5 ch, * in next loop make sc, half dc, 9 dc, half dc and sc; sc in next ch-5 loop, ch 1, picot, ch 2, picot, ch 1, sc in next loop (between the 2 picots), ch 7, sc in next loop (between the 2 picots), ch 1, picot, ch 2, picot, ch 1, sc in next ch-5 loop. Repeat from * around, ending with sc in last loop.

   10th rnd: Sl st in next 3 sts, * ch 5, in center st of same petal make dc, ch 5 and dc; ch 5, skip 3 sts, sc in next st, ch 1, picot, ch 2, picot, ch 1, sc between picots of next loop, ch 7, sc in next ch-7 loop, ch 7, sc in next loop (between picots), ch 1, picot, ch 2, picot, ch 1, skip 2 sts of next petal, sc in next st. Repeat from * around. Join. **11th rnd:** Sl st in next 5 ch, * in next loop make sc, half dc, 9 dc, half dc and sc; sc in next loop, ch 1, picot, ch 2, picot, ch 1, sc between picots of next loop, ch 7, sc in next loop, 7 dc in next sc, sc in next loop, ch 7, sc between picots of next loop, ch 1, picot, ch 2, picot, ch 1, sc in next loop. Repeat from * around, ending with sc in last loop. Join. **12th rnd:** Sl st in next 3 sts, * ch 5, in center st of petal make dc, ch 5 and dc; ch 5, skip 3 sts, sc in next st, ch 1, picot, ch 2, picot, ch 1, sc between picots of next loop, ch 7, sc in next loop, 7 dc in next sc, sc in center dc of next 7-dc group, 7 dc in next sc, sc in next loop, ch 7, sc in next loop, ch 1, picot, ch 2, picot, ch 1, skip 2 sts of next petal, sc in next st. Repeat from * around. Join. **13th rnd:** Sl st in next 5 ch, * in next loop make sc, half dc, 9 dc, half dc and sc; sc in next loop, ch 1, picot, ch 2, picot, ch 1, sc between picots of next loop, ch 7, sc in next loop, (7 dc in next sc, sc in center dc of next 7-dc group) twice; 7 dc in next sc, sc in next loop, ch 7, sc between picots of next loop, ch 1, picot, ch 2, picot, ch 1, sc in next loop. Repeat from * around. Join and break off.

SECOND BLOCK . . . Work as for First Block until 12th rnd is completed. **13th rnd:** Sl st in next 5 ch, in next loop make sc, half dc, 8 dc, sl st in corresponding st of First Block, in same loop of Second Block make dc, half dc and sc; sc in next loop, ch 1, picot, ch 1, sl st in corresponding loop on First Block, ch 1, picot, ch 1, sc between 2 picots of next loop on Second Block, ch 3, sl st in corresponding loop on First Block, ch 3, sc in next loop on Second Block, 4 dc in next sc, sl st in center dc of corresponding dc-group on First Block, 3 dc in same place on Second Block as last 4 dc were made, sc in next loop, complete as for First Block, joining next 2 dc-groups and the following 2 loops to corresponding parts of First Block as before and joining the 1st dc of corner group to corresponding st of First Block.

For Single Size Spread make 13 rows of 20 Blocks. For Double Size Spread make 17 rows of 20 Blocks. Make a row of ch-7 loops around outer edges.

FRINGE . . . *See page 11.*

Irish Crochet Motif

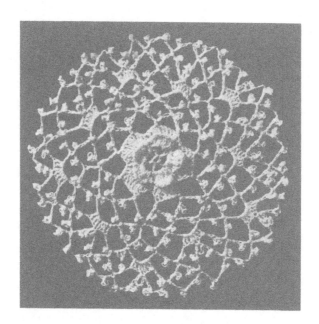

Motif measures about 3½ inches.

Ch 5, join to form a ring.

2nd Row. Ch 6, d c in ring, * ch 3, d c in ring, repeat from * twice.

3rd Row. Ch 1, * 1 d c, 7 tr c, 1 d c in ch 3, 1 s c in d c. repeat from * all around.

4th Row. * Ch 6, s c in next s c in back of petal, repeat from * all around.

5th Row. S c in s c, * 1 d c, 8 tr c, 1 d c in loop, s c in s c, repeat from * all around.

6th Row. Sl st to 2nd tr c, * ch 7, sl st in 5th st from hook for picot, ch 7, sl st in 5th st from hook for picot, ch 2, skip 4 tr c, s c in next tr c, make another double picot ch and s c in 2nd tr c of next petal, repeat from * all around.

7th Row. Sl st to center of loop between picots, * double picot loop, s c between picots of next loop, repeat from * all around.

8th Row. Ch 10, * sl st in 5th st from hook for picot, ch 7, sl st in 5th st from hook for picot, ch 2, s c between picots of next loop, ch 7, s c between picots of next loop, ch 7, sl st in 5th st from hook for picot, ch 7, sl st in 5th st from hook for picot, d c in next s c of last row, ch 7, repeat from * all around and sl st in 3rd st of ch 10.

9th Row. Sl st between next 2 picots, * work a double picot loop, 7 d c over ch 7 of last row, double picot loop, s c between picots of next loop, ch 7, s c between picots of next loop, repeat from * all around.

10th Row. Sl st between picots, * double picot loop, s c in 4th d c, ch 5, s c in same st, double picot loop, s c between picots of next loop, double picot loop, 7 d c over ch 7, double picot loop, s c between picots of next loop and repeat from * all around.

11th Row. Sl st between picots, * double picot loop, s c between picots of next loop, double picot loop, s c between picots of next loop, double picot loop, s c in 4th d c, ch 5, s c in same space, double picot loop, s c between next 2 picots, double picot loop, s c between picots of next loop and repeat from * all around.

Irish Crochet Collar

MATERIALS:

J. & P. COATS or CLARK'S O.N.T. BEST SIX CORD MERCERIZED CROCHET, *Size 50:*

SMALL BALL:

J. & P. COATS—1 ball of White or Ecru,

or

CLARK'S O.N.T.—2 balls of White, Ecru or any color.

Steel Crochet Hook No. 12.

A small pearl button.

Each motif measures about 1½ inches in diameter.

NECKBAND . . . Starting at neck edge, make a chain about 18 inches long (15 ch sts to 1 inch). **1st row:** Sc in 2nd ch from hook, sc in each ch across until there are 233 sc. Ch 2, turn. **2nd row:** Sc in each ch across (233 sc). Ch 2, turn. Repeat 2nd row 2 more times. Do not ch to turn at end of 4th row. **5th row:** Ch 6, sc in 4th ch from hook (p made), ch 5, sc in 4th ch from hook, ch 3 (a p loop made), skip 4 sts, sc in next st, * make a p loop, skip 5 sts, sc in next st. Repeat from * across (39 p loops). Ch 10, turn. **6th row:** Sc in 4th ch from hook, ch 3, sc between p's of next p loop, * make a p loop, sc between p's of next p loop. Repeat from * across, ending with ch 6, p, tr tr in last st of Neckband. Turn. **7th row:** Sl st in p, * make a p loop, sc between p's of next p loop. Repeat from * across, ending with ch 6, p, dc in last p of row below (39 p loops). Fasten off.

FIRST MEDALLION . . . Starting at center, ch 11, join with sl st to form ring. **1st rnd:** Ch 1, 18 sc in ring. Join with sl st in 1st sc. **2nd rnd:** Ch 1, sc in same place as sl st, * ch 5, skip 2 sts, sc in next st. Repeat from * around, joining last ch-5 with sl st in 1st sc (6 loops). **3rd rnd:** In each loop make sc, h dc, 5 dc, h dc and sc. Join. **4th rnd:** * Ch 6, sc in back of next sc on 2nd rnd. Repeat from * around. Join last ch-6 with sl st in first st of first ch-6 (6 loops). **5th rnd:** * In next loop make sc, h dc, 5 dc, h dc and sc; sc in next sc. Repeat from * around. Join. **6th rnd:** * Make a p loop, sc in center dc of next petal, p loop, sc in sc between petals. Repeat from * around. Join with sl st in base of 1st p loop. **7th rnd:** Sl st across to between p's of 1st p loop, ch 6, sc in 4th ch from hook, ch 1, sc in end p loop on Neckband, ch 5, sc in 4th ch from hook, ch 3, sc in next p loop on Medallion, * ch 6, sc in 4th ch from hook, ch 1, sc in next p loop on Neckband, ch 5, sc in 4th ch from hook, ch 3, sc in next p loop on Medallion. Repeat from * once more (3 joinings), finish remainder of rnd with p loops. Fasten off.

SECOND MEDALLION . . . Work as for 1st Medallion until 6th rnd is complete. **7th rnd:** Sl st across to between p's of 1st p loop, ch 6, sc in 4th ch from hook, ch 1, sc in 2nd p loop (from last joining) on 1st Medallion, join next p loop to next p loop on 1st Medallion and following 3 p loops to next 3 p loops on Neckband, finish rnd with no more joinings. Fasten off.

Make 11 more medallions, joining them as 2nd Medallion was joined to 1st. Fasten off.

Brush medallions lightly with starch and press. Make a ch-7 buttonloop on right back edge of collar. Sew on button to correspond,

Irish Popcorn Bedspread

The combination of Irish Crochet with the tufted popcorn stitch in this bedspread is very effective, especially when it is made in soft gleaming Knit-Cro-Sheen.

MATERIALS:

I Milward's steel crochet hook No. 6 or 7

Choose one of the following threads in White or Ecru:

J. & P. Coats Knit-Cro-Sheen (approx. 76 balls)

Clark's O.N.T. Lustersheen (approx. 58 skeins)

Clark's O.N.T. Knitting and Crochet Cotton (approx. 58 balls)

This amount is sufficient for a double size spread.

Gauge: Each block measures about 5 inches square and requires about 57 yards of thread. For a double size spread (about 98 x 113 inches) or a single size spread (about 78 x 113 inches), make the necessary amount of blocks and then join them together to correspond with measurement.

Block. To begin, ch 8, join with sl st to form a ring. **1st row:** Ch 1, 12 s c in ring. Join with sl st in 1st s c. **2nd row:** * Ch 5, skip 1 s c, 1 s c in next s c. Repeat from * until there are 6 loops. Join the last ch 5 in the s c of the first loop. **3rd row:** Over each ch-5 work 1 s c, 1 half d c, 5 d c, 1 half d c, 1 s c. **4th row:** Ch 5, fasten with s c on back of preceding row between two petals, ch 5, fasten as before. Repeat around 6 petals. **5th row:** Over each ch-5 work 1 s c, 1 half d c, 1 d c, 5 tr, 1 d c, 1 half d c, 1 s c.

6th row: Sl st in each of first 3 sts of 1st petal made in this row, 1 s c in 1st tr, * ch 9, 1 s c in 5th tr, ch 4, 1 s c in same st forming a p, ch 7, 1 s c and 1 p in 1st tr of next petal, ch 7, 1 s c and 1 p in 5th tr, ch 9, 1 s c and 1 p in 1st tr of next petal, ch 7, 1 s c and 1 p in 5th tr of same petal, ch 7, 1 s c and 1 p in 1st tr of next petal, and repeat from * once. **7th row:** Sl st to middle of ch-9 loop, * ch 7, 1 s c in same st from which ch-7 started, ch 7, 1 s c and 1 p in center of next ch-7 loop of preceding row, ch 7, 1 s c and 1 p in center of next ch-7 loop, ch 7, 1 s c in center of ch-9 and repeat from * 3 times.

8th row: Sl st to middle of 1st ch-7 loop, ch 8, 1 d c in same st from which ch-8 started, * ch 6, 1 s c and 1 p in center of ch of preceding row, ch 7, 1 s c and 1 p in center of next ch-7, ch 7, 1 s c and 1 p in center of next ch-7, ch 6, 1 c c in center of next ch-7 loop, ch 5, 1 d c in same st from which ch-5 started and repeat from * 3 times, ending row with sl st (instead of d c) in 3rd st of ch-8. **9th row:** Ch 3, * 1 d c in each of the next 2 sts, ch 5, 1 d c in same st as previous d c, 1 d c in each of the next 2 sts, 1 popcorn st in next st as follows: ch 1, 5 d c in next d c, drop st from hook, insert hook back in ch-1 and draw dropped loop through the one on hook. 1 d c in each of the next 3 sts, ch 6, 1 s c and p in center of ch loop of preceding row, ch 7, 1 s c and 1 p in center of next ch loop, ch 6, 1 d c in each of last 3 sts of next ch-6, 1 popcorn st in next d c, 1 d c in next st. Repeat from * 3 times, ending row with a popcorn st and sl st in 3rd st of ch-3 first made.

10th row: Ch 3,* 1 d c in next d c, 1 popcorn st, 1 d c in each of the next 3 sts, ch 5, 1 d c in same st for corner. Work in next 12 sts as follows: 2 d c, 1 popcorn st, 5 d c, 1 popcorn st, 3 d c (catching hook in back loop only throughout block) ch 6,1 s c and 1 p in center of next ch loop, ch 6, 1 d c in center of next ch loop, 2 d c, 1 popcorn st, 5 d c, 1 popcorn st, 4 d c. Repeat from * 3 times, ending row by sl st in 3rd st of ch-3 first made. **11 th row:** Ch 3, * 4 d c, 1 popcorn st, 3 d c, ch 5, 1 d c in same st for corner. Work in next 18 sts—2 d c, 1 popcorn st, 5 d c, 1 popcorn st, 5 d c, 1 popcorn st, 3 d c. Ch 5, 1 d c in center of next ch loop, 2 d c, 1 popcorn st, 5 d c, 1 popcorn st, 1 d c and repeat from * 3 times, ending row with popcorn st and sl st in 3rd st of ch-3 first made.

12th row: Ch 3, 1 d c in each st to corner, ch 5, 1 d c in same st for corner, then 1 d c in each st making corners as before. Join with sl st in 3rd st of ch-3 first made. **13th row:** Ch 3, skip 2 sts, 1 s c in next st. Continue around entire block with ch 3 and s c so that there are 18 loops on each side and an additional loop at each corner.

To join, catch with s c on ch-3 nearest the edge, ch 3, catch with s c in same position on 2nd block, ch 3, 1 s c on next ch-3 of 1st block, ch 3, catch on 2nd block and so on along one side.

Outer edge—1st **row:** Ch 7 and s c in alternate ch-3's. **2nd row:** Ch 7 and 1 p in each loop.

Make a fringe into each loop all around bedspread.

To make fringe, turn to page 11.

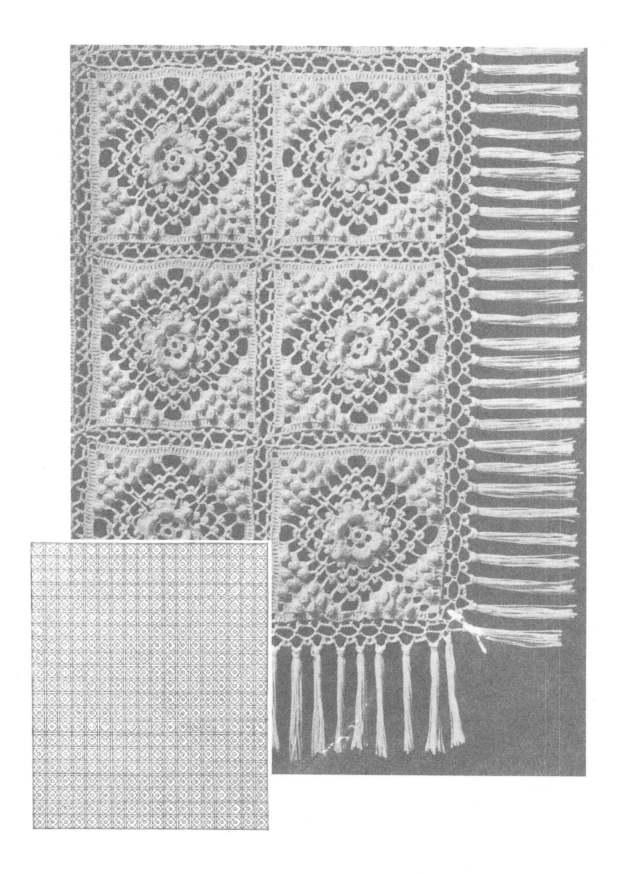

Rose of sharon

MATERIALS:

J. & P. COATS TATTING COTTON, *4 balls of White, Ecru, or any color.*

Steel Crochet Hook No. 14.

Doily measures about 10½ inches in diameter.

Starting at center, ch 10, join with sl st. **1st rnd:** 24 sc in ring, sl st in 1st sc made. **2nd rnd:** Sc in same place as sl st, * ch 5, skip 3 sc, sc in next sc. Repeat from * around. Sl st in 1st sc made (6 loops made). **3rd rnd:** In each loop make sc, half dc, 3 dc, half dc and sc. Sl st in 1 st sc made (6 petals made). **4th rnd:** Ch 5, 1 sc between petals with ch 5 between sc's. Join (6 loops made). **5th rnd:** Repeat 3rd rnd. **6th rnd:** Sl st between sc and half dc, ch 7, to count as d tr and 2-ch, * d tr between half dc and dc, (ch 2, d tr between this dc and next dc) twice; ch 2, d tr between this dc and next half dc, ch 2, d tr between this half dc and next sc, ch 2, skip 2 sc and half dc, make d tr between this half dc and next dc, (ch 2, d tr between this dc and next dc) twice; ch 2, d tr between this dc and next half dc, ch 2, d tr between this half dc and next sc, ch 2, skip 2 sc, make d tr between last sc and next half dc, ch 2. Repeat from * around, ending with d tr between last half dc and sc of 6th petal, sl st in 5th ch of ch-7 (33 d tr, counting starting ch as 1 d tr). **7th rnd:** Sl st in next ch-2 sp, sc in same sp, * ch 4, sc in next sp. Repeat from * around, ending with sc in 1st loop made. **8th and 9th rnds:** * Ch 5, sc in next, loop. Repeat from * around, ending with sc in 1st loop made. **10th rnd:** Same as 9th rnd, but making ch-6 loops instead of ch-5. **11th rnd:** * (Ch 4, dc in 4th ch from hook) twice; sc in next loop (a 2-group loop made). Repeat from * around, ending with sc in last loop before 1st group. **12th rnd:** * (Ch 4, dc in 4th ch from hook) 4 times; sc between 1st and 2nd groups just made, ch 4, dc in 4th ch from hook, sc between next 2 groups of previous rnd (a 5-group loop made); (ch 4, dc in 4th ch from hook) twice; sc between next 2 groups of previous rnd. Repeat from * 15 more times. Fasten off. **13th rnd:** *Leaves are made individually as follow:*

First Leaf . . . 1st row: Starting at center ch 11, sc in 2nd ch from hook and in each ch across, ch 2, sc in same place as last sc, sc in each ch along opposite side of foundation chain. Ch 1, turn. Hereafter, pick up only the back loop of each sc throughout. **2nd row:** Sc in each sc across to within the ch-2 sp; in the sp work sc, ch 2 and sc, then work sc in each sc along other side to within last sc, ch 1, turn (1 sc decreased).

Repeat 2nd row until there are 14 sc on each side of ch-2 sp. Ch 1., turn. To join, work sc in 9 sc, sc between 2nd and 3rd groups of a 5-group loop, sc in each remaining sc on leaf to within the ch-2 sp, sc in sp, ch 1, sc between the 2 groups of next 2-group loop on center, ch 1, sc back in ch-2 sp of leaf, sc in next 5 sc, sc between 3rd and 4th groups of next 5-group loop, sc in next 9 sc on leaf. Fasten off.

Second Leaf . . . Work same as First Leaf until there are 14 sc on each side of ch-2 sp, but join as follows: Ch 1, sc in last sc of previous leaf, turn; sc in next 9 sc on Second Leaf, sc between 2nd and 3rd groups of same 5-group loop to which previous leaf was joined. Sc in each remaining sc on Second Leaf to within the ch-2 sp, sc in sp, ch 1, sc between the 2 groups of next 2-group loop on center, ch 1, sc back in ch-2 sp of leaf, and complete joining in same way that First Leaf was joined. Fasten off. Make 14 more leaves like this, joining as Second Leaf was joined, and joining last leaf with sc to First Leaf to complete 13th rnd of doily. Do not fasten off. **14th rnd:** Ch 3, skip 1 row of last leaf, * dc at end of next row, * (ch 4, dc in 4th ch from hook) twice; skip 3 rows of same leaf, sc at end of next row. Repeat from * 2 more times, (ch 4, dc in 4th ch from hook) twice; dc in last row of same leaf, skip 1 row of next leaf. Repeat from * * around, ending with sc between the 2 groups of 1st loop made. **15th and 16th rnds:** * (Ch 4, dc in 4th ch from hook) twice; sc in center of next loop. Repeat from * around. Fasten off.

17th rnd: *Motif, are made individually as follows:*

First Rosette Motif . . . Repeat first 6 rnds of doily. **7th rnd:** Sl st in next ch-2 sp; sc in same sp, * ch 3, sc in next sp. Repeat from * around, ending with sl st in 1st sc made (33 loops). 8th rnd: Sl st to center of next loop, sc in same loop, * ch 3, sc in next loop. Repeat from around. Join. **9th rnd:** Sl st to center of next loop, ch 7, to count as dc and 3-ch, sc in 3rd ch from hook (a p made); ch 1, (dc in same loop, p, ch 1) twice; dc in same loop, ch 5, skip 3 loops; in next loop make 4 dc with p and ch-1 between (a shell made); ch 2, sc in center of loop on last rnd of doily, * ch 2, skip 2 loops on motif, in next loop make dc, p, ch 1 and dc; ch 1, sc in center of next loop on doily, ch 1, dc back in same loop as last dc on motif, p, ch 1, dc in same place on motif. Repeat from * once more. Ch 2, sc in center of next loop on doily, ch 2, skip 2 loops on motif, make a shell in next loop, ch 5, skip 3 loops, make a shell in next loop, (p, ch 2, p, ch 1, skip 3 loops, make shell in next loop) 3 times; p, ch 2, p, ch 1, join with sl st to 3rd ch of ch-7 first made. Fasten off.

First Petal Motif . . . Starting at center, ch 12. Join. **1st rnd:** Ch 3, 23 dc in ring, sl st in top of ch-3 first made. **2nd rnd:** Ch 4, to count as dc and 1 ch, * dc in next dc, ch 1. Repeat from * around, sl st in 3rd st of ch-4. **3rd rnd:** * * Sl st in next sp, ch 9, dc in 4th ch from hook and in each ch across, sc in next sp of previous rnd, ch 2, turn. Working along petal, make half dc between 1st and 2nd dc, * half dc between this and next dc. Repeat from * across one side, make 5 half dc at tip of petal, then work across opposite side to correspond, sl st into sp, ch 1, turn. Sc in each half dc to tip of petal, 3 sc in center half dc, sc in each half dc across other side, sc in next sp of previous rnd (1 petal made). Repeat from * * until 8 petals have been made in all. Fasten off. **4th rnd:** Attach thread in 3rd sc down from tip at left side of 1 petal, ch 3, dc in corresponding sc of next petal, ch 4, sl st in center of second shell from joining on Rosette Motif; ch 3, sc at tip of same petal on Petal Motif; ch 3, skip 2 ch on Rosette Motif, sc in next ch. Ch 4, dc in 3rd sc down from tip of same petal, dc in corresponding sc of next petal, ch 3, sl st in center of next shell on Rosette Motif; ch 5, sc in tip of same petal, * sl st in center of next loop on doily, sl st in next 3 sc of petal, ch 3, sl st in center of next loop on doily; ch 3, sl st in corresponding sc of next petal, sl st to tip of same petal. Repeat from * once more. Sl st in center of next loop on doily, ch 8, dc in 3rd sc down from tip of same petal, dc in corresponding sc of next petal, ch 7, sc in tip of same petal, ch 7, ** dc in 3rd sc down from tip of same petal, dc in corresponding sc of next petal, ch 1, p, ch 1, shell at tip of same petal, ch 1, p, ch 2. Repeat from * until 3 shells are made, ch 1, p, ch 2, sl st in 3rd ch of ch 3 first made. Fasten off.

Alternate Rosette and Petal Motifs, joining as first 2 motifs were joined (14 motifs in all). Join last motif on both sides.

FRINGE

Plain Fringe: Cut 10 strands of thread, each 12 inches long. Double these strands to form a loop (Fig. 1). Insert hook (Fig. 2) in space on edge of bedspread and draw loop through (Fig. 3). Draw loose ends through loop (Fig. 4) and pull up tightly to form a knot (Fig. 5). Make a fringe in every other space (or every half inch) around spread. When fringe is completed, trim ends evenly.

Knotted Fringe: Cut 8 strands of thread, each 16 inches long, and make a Plain Fringe around edges of spread (Figs. 1-5). Pick up 8 strands of the first fringe and 8 strands of the second fringe and make a knot (Fig. 6) 1 inch down and in the center between 2 previous knots. Pick up remaining strands of second fringe and first 8 strands of next fringe and knot as before. Continue in this manner around. Trim ends evenly.

Fig. 1

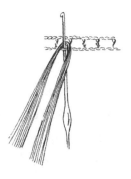

Fig. 2

Fig. 3

Fig. 4

Fig. 5

Fig. 6

Irish Crochet Doily

MATERIALS:

CLARK'S O.N.T. or J. & P. COATS BEST SIX CORD MERCERIZED CROCHET, size 50:

CLARK' S O.N.T.—4 balls of White or Ecru, or 5 balls of color,

OR

J. & P. COATS—2 balls of White or Ecru.

Steel crochet hook No. 12.

Completed doily measures about 11 inches in diameter.

LARGE FLOWER . . . Ch 20. **1st row:** Sc in 2nd ch from hook, sc in each ch across, 3 sc in end ch, sc in each ch along other side of foundation ch. Ch 1, turn. Hereafter pick up back loop only of each sc. **2nd row:** Sc in each sc to within 3 sc at tip, 2 sc in each of 3 tip sts, sc in each sc to end of row. Ch 4, turn. **3rd row:** Skip the sc at base of ch and next 3 sc, sc in next sc, (ch 4, skip 3 sc, sc in next sc) 3 times; (ch 4, skip 2 sc, sc in next sc) 3 times; (ch 4, skip 3 sc, sc in next sc) 4 times. Fasten off. This completes one petal. Work 1st 2 rows of a 2nd petal as for 1st petal, ending with ch 2, turn. **3rd row:** Sl st in end loop of 1st petal, ch 2, skip 3 sc on 2nd petal, sc in next sc, ch 2, sl st in corresponding loop of 1st petal, ch 2, skip 3 sc, sc in next sc, ch 4 and complete this petal same as 1st petal (no more joinings). Make 10 more petals, joining 2 loops of adjacent petals as before (join last 2 loops of last petal to 1st 2 loops of 1st petal). Fasten off. Attach thread to base of any petal and working toward center make 2 sc-rnds, one dc-rnd and 1 sc-rnd, decreasing as necessary to keep work flat by working off 2 sts as one.

ROSETTE . . . Ch 10, join. **1st rnd:** * In ring make sc, h dc, 5 dc, h dc and sc. Repeat from * 4 more times (5 petals). **2nd rnd:** * Ch 6, then inserting hook from behind petals, work sc in ring between next 2 sc. Repeat from * around (5 loops). **3rd rnd:** In each loop make sc, h dc, dc, 8 tr, dc, h dc and sc. Sl st in 1st sc made. Fasten off. Sew this rosette to center of Flower.

LEAF . . . Starting at tip, ch 15. **1st row:** Sc in 2nd ch from hook, sc in each ch to within last ch, 3 sc in last ch, sc in each ch along opposite side of foundation ch, sc in same place as last sc. Mark last sc for base of leaf. Hereafter pick up only the back loop of each sc. Do not turn, but work sc in each sc to within 3 sc from center sc at tip of leaf. Ch 1, turn. **2nd row:** Sc in each sc to marked sc, 3 sc in marked sc, sc in each sc on other side to within 3 sc from center sc at tip of leaf. Ch 1, turn. **3rd and 4th rows:** Sc in each sc to within center sc of 3-sc group, 3 sc in next sc, sc in each sc on other side to within last 3 sts. Ch 1, turn. **5th row:** Same as 3rd row but making sc, ch 7 and sc in center sc of sc-group at base of leaf. **6th row:** Sc in each sc to within ch-7 loop; 2 sc in loop, then pick up Flower and holding Flower away from you, join leaf between 2 petals as follows: Ch 2, sl st in 1st loop to left of loop at tip of a petal, ch 2, 3 sc in ch-7 loop, ch 5, 3 sc in same loop, ch 2, sl st in corresponding loop of next petal, ch 2, 2 sc in ch-7 loop, sc in back loop of each sc across to within last 3 sts. Fasten off. Make 11 more leaves, joining each leaf between 2 petals of Flower as 1st leaf was joined. Attach thread to loop at tip of a petal, * ch 7, sc in 1st corner st of adjacent leaf, (ch 7, sc in next corner st of same leaf) twice; ch 7, at tip of leaf make sc, ch 7 and sc; (ch 7, sc in next corner st of leaf) 3 times; ch 7, sc in loop at tip of next petal. Repeat from * around. Join and fasten off.

Work a rosette as for center, but do not break off. Work sl st in next 4 sts, sc in next st, ch 7, skip 3 sts, sc in next st, then pick up doily and join rosette between 2 leaves as follows: Ch 3, tr in loop at tip of leaf, ch 3, sc in 5th st of next petal of rosette, ch 3, skip next loop on leaf, sl st in next loop, ch 3, skip 3 sts on rosette, sc in next st, ch 3, then holding back on hook the last loop of each tr make tr in next loop on leaf and in corresponding loop on next leaf, thread over and draw through all loops on hook; ch 3, sc in the 5th st of next petal, ch 3, sl st in next loop on leaf, ch 3, skip 3 sts on petal, sc in next st, ch 3, tr in loop at tip of leaf, ch 3, sc in 5th st of next petal,

* ch 7, skip 3 sts, sc in next st, ch 7, sc in 5th st of next petal. Repeat from * once more. Join and fasten off. Make and join 11 more rosettes in same way. Now work a rnd of loops as follows: Attach thread to tr-bar at right of loop which is at tip of leaf, ch 4, tr under next tr (at left of leaf), ** ch 3, sc in 3rd st from hook (p made), ch 2, sc in next free loop on rosette, * ch 2, p, ch 2, p, ch 2, sc in next loop. Repeat from * 3 more times; ch 2, p, then holding back on hook the last loop of each tr make tr under next 2 tr, thread over and draw through all loops on hook. Repeat from ** around. Join last p with sl st to 4th st of ch-4. Fasten off. Work a leaf as before until the 5th row

is completed. **6th row:** Sc in each sc to within ch-7 loop; 2 sc in loop, then pick up doily and join as follows: Ch 2, sl st in 2nd p preceding joined tr's between rosettes, ch 2, 3 sc in ch-7 loop of leaf, ch 5, 3 sc in same loop, ch 2, sl st in 2nd p after same joined tr's, ch 2, 2 sc in ch-7 loop and complete leaf as before. Make and join 11 more leaves in this manner. Make another leaf until the 5th row is completed. **6th row:** Sc in each sc to within ch-7 loop, in loop work 2 sc, ch 5, and 3 sc. Ch 2, sl st in sc above center petal of rosette, ch 2, 3 sc in ch-7 loop, ch 5, 2 sc in same loop, and complete leaf as before. Make and join 11 more leaves in this manner.

Now work 3 rnds of loops as follows: **1st rnd:** Attach thread to tip of a leaf which is joined between rosettes, ch 7, sc in same place, * (ch 7, sc in next corner st) 3 times; tr in next free loop of rosette, tr in free loop of next leaf, (ch 7, sc in next corner st) 3 times; ch 7, in tip of leaf make sc, ch 7 and sc; (ch 7, sc in next corner st) 3 times; ch 7, tr in free loop of leaf, tr in next free loop of rosette, sc in next corner st of next leaf, (ch 7, sc in next corner st) twice; ch 7, in tip of leaf make sc, ch 7 and sc. Repeat from * around, ending with ch 7, sl st where thread was attached. **2nd rnd:** Sl st in next 3 ch, sc in loop, (ch 2, p, ch 2, p, ch 2, sc in next loop) twice; * ch 2, p, holding back on hook the last loop of each tr make tr in each of next 2 ch-7 loops, thread over and draw through all loops on hook, p, ch 2, sc in next ch-7 loop, (ch 2, p, ch 2, p, ch 2, sc in next loop) 6 times; ch 2, p, then holding back on hook the last loop of each tr, work tr in next 2 ch-7 loops, thread over and draw through all loops on hook; p, ch 2, sc in next loop, (ch 2, p, ch 2, p, ch 2, sc in next loop) 4 times. Repeat from * around. Join last loop with sl st to 1st sc made. **3rd rnd:** Sl st to center of next loop, sc in loop, ch 2, p, ch 2, p and ch 2; sc in next loop, * ch 3, sc between p's of next free loop, (ch 2, p, ch 2, p and ch 2, sc in next loop) 5 times; ch 3, sc between p's of next free loop, (ch 2, p, ch 2, p, ch 2, sc in next loop) 3 times. Repeat from * around. Join and fasten off.

Irish Crochet Trim

Materials suggested: American Thread Company "Silkine" or "Star" Mercerized 6 Cord Crochet Cotton sizes 30 to 70 or "Silkine" Tatting Cotton, White or Colors.

Ch 6, join to form a ring, * ch 5, d c in ring, ch 3, d c in ring, repeat from * 6 times and work 1 s c, 4 d c, 1 s c in each loop. Carry thread in back of petal and join to d c of 1st row, ch 8, d c in next d c, ch 4, d c in next d c, repeat all around and work 1 s c, 5 d c, 1 s c in each loop. Sl st to center of petal, ch 6, sl st in 4th st for picot, ch 3, s c in center of next petal, repeat picot loops all around. Sl st to center of ch, * work a picot loop, s c in ch on other side of picot, picot loop, s c in next ch, ch 6, turn, s c in next s c, ch 3, 7 d c over loop, picot loop, s c in next ch, picot loop, s c in next ch, repeat from * all around and work another row of picot loops. Work as many motifs as required joining them at picots as illustrated.

SCALLOP. Begin between scallops, ch 4, sl st in next picot, repeat across row, turn, 5 s c over 6 loops, turn, * ch 6, sl st in s c over picot, repeat from * 3 times, turn and work 9 s c over each loop, 5 s c over last 2 loops and repeat from beginning for entire length. Straight edge of lace: D tr c between scallops, ch 3 * s1 st in picot, ch 3, repeat from * 5 times and from beginning for entire length. Finish with one row of s c.

Irish Rose Tablecloth

What You Need:
ROYAL SOCIETY SIX CORD CORDICHET
Small Ball, size 30:
114 balls.
OR
Large Ball, size 30:
36 balls.
Steel Crochet Hook No. 10 or 11.

Tablecloth measures about 70 x 106 inches, including the edging.

GAUGE: Motif measures about 3 inches square after blocking.

FIRST MOTIF . . . Starting at center, ch 6. Join with sl st to form ring. **1st rnd:** Ch 5, * dc in ring, ch 2. Repeat from * 4 more times. Sl st in 3rd st of ch-5 (6 sps). **2nd rnd:** In each sp around make sc, h dc, 3 dc, h dc and sc (6 petals). **3rd rnd:** * Ch 5, insert hook in next sp (from back of work) and in following sp (from front of work), thread over and draw loop through, thread over and draw through both loops on hook. Repeat from * around (6 sps). **4th rnd:** In each sp around, make sc, h dc, 7 dc, h dc and sc. **5th rnd:** * Ch 6, insert hook in next sp (from back of work) and in next sp (from front of work), thread over and draw loop through, thread over and draw through both loops on hook. Repeat from * around (6 sps). **6th rnd:** 8 sc in each sp around (48 sc on rnd). **7th rnd:** Ch 1. * sc in next sc, ch 3, dc in next sc, (ch 1, tr in next sc) 4 times; ch 1, dc in next sc, ch 3, sc in next sc. Repeat from * around. Sl st in 1st sc made.

8th rnd: Ch 11 (to count as tr and ch 7), sc in 3rd ch from hook (p made), ch 1, * sc in center ch-1 sp of petal, ch 1, p, ch 4, tr in 1st sc of next petal, ch 5, sc in center ch-1 sp of petal, ch 4, p, ch 1, tr in 1st sc of next petal, ch I, p, ch 4, sc in center ch-1 sp of petal, ch 5, tr in 1st sc of next petal, ch 4, p, ch 1. Repeat from * around, ending with ch 5, sl st in 4th st of ch-11 first made. **9th rnd:** Sl st to center of next loop, sc in loop, ch 1, p, ch 2, p, ch 1, sc in next loop, * ch 1, p, ch 4, in next loop make cluster, ch 5 and cluster—to *make a cluster, holding back the last loop of each tr on hook make 3 tr in same place, thread over and draw through all loops on hook;* ch 4, p, ch 1, sc in next loop, ch 1, p, ch 2, p, ch 1, sc in next loop. Repeat from * around. Sl st in 1st sc made. **10th rnd:** Sl st to center of next loop, sc in loop, ch 1, p, ch 2, p, ch 1, sc in next loop, * ch 1, p, ch 4, in corner loop make cluster, ch 5 and cluster; ch 4, p, ch 1, sc in next loop, (ch 1, p, ch 2, p, ch 1, sc in next loop) twice. Repeat from * around. Join. 11th rnd: Sl st to center of next loop, sc in loop, ch 1, p, ch 2, p, ch 1, sc in next loop, * ch 1, p, ch 4, in next corner loop make cluster, ch 13 and cluster; ch 4, p, ch 1, sc in next loop, (ch 1, p, ch 2, p, ch 1, sc in next loop) 3 times. Repeat from * around. Join and fasten off.

SECOND MOTIF . . . Work as for 1st motif to 10th rnd incl. **11th rnd:** Work as for 11th rnd of 1st motif to within 1st cluster; make cluster in corner loop, ch 6, sc in corner loop of 1st motif, ch 6, cluster in same corner loop on motif in work, ch 3, sc in corresponding loop on 1st motif, ch 1, p, ch I, sc in next loop on motif in work, ch 1, p, ch 1, sc in corresponding loop on 1st motif, ch 1, p, ch 1, sc in next loop on motif in work. Join next 2 loops to corresponding loops of 1st motif in same way, ch 1, p, ch 1, sc in corresponding loop on 1st motif, ch 3, cluster in corner loop on motif in work, ch 6, sc in corner loop on 1st motif, ch 6, cluster in same loop on motif in work and complete rnd as for 1st motif (no more joinings).

Make 22 x 34 motifs, joining adjacent sides as 2nd motif was joined to 1st (where 4 corners meet, join 3rd and 4th corners to joining of previous two).

EDGING ... 1st rnd: Attach thread to corner loop on a corner motif, ch 4, in same loop make tr, ch 5 and 2 tr; * (ch 5, 2 tr in next loop) 5 times; ch 5, tr in next loop (preceding joining), tr in next loop (following joining). Repeat from * around. Join last ch 5 to 4th st of ch-4. **2nd, 3rd and 4th rnds:** Sl st in next tr and the following 3 ch, ch 4, tr in same place as sl st, * ch 5, tr in next 2 tr. Repeat from * around, making 2 tr, ch 5 and 2 tr in center st of each corner ch-5. Join. **5th rnd:** Sl st in next tr and in next loop, ch 4, holding back the last loop of each tr make 2 tr in same loop and complete cluster, (ch 5, cluster in same loop) twice; * ch 1, p, ch 1, sc in next sp, ch 1, p, ch 1, in next sp make cluster, ch 5 and cluster. Repeat from * around, making 3 clusters with ch 5 between in each corner loop, and ending with ch 1, p, ch 1; sl st in tip of 1st cluster made. **6th rnd:** Sl st in next loop, ch 4 and complete cluster as before, (ch 1, p, ch 1, cluster in same loop as last cluster) twice; ch 3, sc in tip of next cluster, ch 3, in next loop make (cluster, ch 1, p, ch 1) twice, and cluster; ch 3, sc in next loop (preceding p), * ch 5, sc in next loop (following p), ch 3, in next loop make (cluster, ch 1, p, ch 1) twice and cluster; ch 3, sc in next loop. Repeat from * around, working over corner as before, and ending with ch 3; sl st in tip of 1st cluster made. Fasten off.

Cinderella Bedspread

How simple to transform a drab room into one of colorful beauty. We have added a simple edging and band of Irish Crochet to a yellow organdy spread. Why not trim a white spread with Cherry Red trimming— add curtains and dressing table to match?

This Spread may be made with any of the
AMERICAN THREAD COMPANY products listed below:

Materials	QUANTITY
"STAR" CROCHET COTTON ARTICLE 20 Size 30	27 Balls Yellow or any Color desired
or	
"STAR" CROCHET COTTON ARTICLE 30 Size 30	83 Balls
or	
"GEM" CROCHET COTTON ARTICLE 35 Size 30	22 Balls
and	
"STAR" MERCERIZED SEWING THREAD — ARTICLE 400	2 Spools

Yellow Organdie Spread 40 x 88 inches without Ruffle and I Sham Top.

Each Motif measures 3 inches. Steel Crochet Hook No. 12.

MOTIF: Ch 5, join to form a ring, * ch 4, s c in ring, repeat from * 3 times.

2nd Row. Sl st into loop, ch 1 and work 1 s c, 5 d c, I s c over each loop.

3rd Row. * Ch 3 and working in back of petals, work 1 s c in center d c of next petal, ch 3, s c between next 2 petals, repeat from * 3 times.

4th Row. 1 s c, 7 d c, 1 s c over each loop.

5th Row. * Ch 5, s c in back of work between next 2 petals, repeat from * all around.

6th Row. 1 s c, 9 d c, 1 s c over each loop.

7th Row. Ch 7, s c in center d c of next petal, * ch 4, d c between next 2 petals, ch 4, s c in center d c of next petal, repeat from * all around ending row with ch 4, sl st in 3rd st of ch.

8th Row. * Ch 7, s c in next s c, ch 7, s c in next d c, repeat from * all around.

9th Row. Sl st into loop, ch 4 (counts as ⅓ part of 1st tr c cluster st) , * thread over hook twice, insert in same loop, pull through and work off 2 loops twice, repeat from * once, thread over and work off all loops at one time, ** ch 3, tr c cluster st in same space (tr c cluster st: * thread over hook twice, insert in same space, pull through and work off 2 loops twice, repeat from * twice, thread over and work off all loops at one time) , repeat from ** once, ** ch 5, s c in next loop, ch 4, 2 d c cluster sts with ch 3 between in next loop, (d c cluster st: thread over hook once, insert in loop, pull through and work off 2 loops, * thread over hook once, insert in same space, pull through and work off 2 loops, repeat from * once., thread over and work off remaining loops at one time) , ch 4, s c in next loop, ch 5, 3 tr c cluster sts with ch 3 between each tr c cluster st in next loop, repeat from last ** twice, ch 5, s c in next loop, ch 4, 2 d c cluster sts with ch 3 between in next loop, ch 4, s c in next loop, ch 5, sl st in top of 1st cluster st.

10th Row. Sl st to center tr c cluster st of 3 tr c cluster st group and work 2 tr c cluster sts with ch 7 between in same space, * ch 5, skip next loop, s c in next loop, ch 4, s c in next loop, ch 3, 2 d c cluster sts with ch 3 between in next loop, ch 3, s c in next loop, ch 4, s c in next loop, ch 5, 2 tr c cluster sts with ch 7 between in center cluster st of next cluster st group, repeat from * twice, ch 5, skip l loop, s c in next loop, ch 4, s c in next loop, ch 3, 2 d c cluster sts with ch 3 between in next loop, ch 3, s c in next loop, ch 4, s c in next loop, ch 5, join in top of 1st cluster st.

11th Row. Ch 7, tr c cluster st in next loop, ch 3, sl st in top of cluster st for picot, ch 7, s c in next cluster st, ch 5, tr c cluster st in next s c, ch 3, sl st in top of cluster st for picot, ch 5, s c in next loop, ch 5, skip 1 loop, s c in next loop, ch 3, sl st in top of s c for picot, ch 5, skip 1 loop, s c in next loop, ch 5, tr c cluster st in next s c, ch 3, sl st in top of cluster st for picot, ch 5, skip 1 loop, s c in next cluster st, repeat from beginning all around, break thread. Work another motif in same manner joining to 1st motif in last row as follows: ch 7, tr c cluster st in next loop, ch 1, sl st in corresponding picot of 1st motif, ch 1, complete picot, ch 7, s c in next cluster st of 2nd motif, ch 5, tr c cluster st in next s c of 2nd motif, ch 1, sl st in corresponding picot of 1st motif, ch 1, complete picot, ch 5, s c in next loop of 2nd motif, ch 5, skip 1 loop, s c in next loop, ch 1, sl st in corresponding picot of 1st motif, ch 1, complete picot, ch 5, skip 1 loop of 2nd motif, s c in next loop, ch 5, tr c cluster st in next s c, ch 1, sl st in corresponding picot of 1st motif, ch 1, complete picot, ch 5, skip 1 loop of 2nd motif, s c in next cluster st, ch 7, tr c cluster st in next loop, ch 1, sl st in corresponding picot of 1st motif, ch 1, complete picot, complete motif same as 1st motif. Join all motifs in same manner following chart.

HALF MOTIF: Ch 5, join to form a ring, * ch 4, s c in ring, repeat from * once, ch 1, turn.

2nd Row. 1 s c, 5 d c, 1 s c over each loop, ch 3, turn.

3rd Row. Working in back of petals work 1 s c in center d c of next petal, ch 3, s c between next 2 petals, ch 3, s c in center d c of next petal, ch 3, s c in end s c, ch 1, turn.

4th Row. 1 s c, 7 d c, 1 s c over each loop, ch 5, turn.

5th Row. S c in back of work between next 2 petals, * ch 5, s c in back of work between next 2 petals, repeat from * once, ch 5, s c in end s c, ch 1, turn.

6th Row. 1 s c, 9 d c , 1 s c c over each loop, ch 7, turn.

7th Row. S c in center d c of next petal, ch 4, d c between next 2 petals, ch 4, repeat from beginning once, d c in same space, ch 4, s c in center d c of next petal, ch 4, d c between next 2 petals, ch 4, s c in center d c of next petal, ch 4, d c in end s c, ch 7, turn.

8th Row. S c in next s c, ch 7, s c in next d c, ch 7, s c in next s c, * ch 7, s c in next d c, repeat from * once, ch 7, s c in next s c, ch 7, s c in next d c, ch 7, s c in next s c, ch 7, s c in 3rd st of ch, turn.

9th Row. Ch 4 and work 2 tr c cluster sts with ch 3 between in 1st loop, ch 5, s c in next loop, ch 4, 2 d c cluster sts with ch 3 between in next loop, ch 4, s c in next loop, ch 5, 3 tr c cluster sts with ch 3 between each cluster st in next loop, ch 5, s c in next loop, ch 4, 2 d c cluster sts with ch 3 between in next loop, ch 4, s c in next loop, ch 5, 2 tr c cluster sts with ch 3 between in next loop, turn.

10th Row. 2 tr c cluster sts with ch 7 between in top of 1st cluster st, ch 5, skip 1 loop, s c in next loop, ch 4, s c in next loop, ch 3, 2 d c cluster sts with ch 3 between in next loop, ch 3, s c in next loop, ch 4, s c in next loop, ch 5, 2 tr c cluster sts with ch 7 between in center tr c cluster st of 3 tr c cluster st group, ch 5, skip 1 loop, s c in next loop, ch 4, s c in next loop, ch 3, 2 d c cluster sts with ch 3 between in next loop, ch 3, s c in next loop, ch 4, s c in next loop, ch 5, skip 1 loop, 2 tr c cluster sts with ch 7 between in end cluster st, turn.

11th Row. Ch 7, tr c cluster st in 1st loop, ch 1, sl st in corner picot of motif, ch 1, complete picot, ch 7, s c in next cluster st of half motif, ch 5, tr c cluster st in next s c, ch 1, sl st in corresponding picot of motif, ch 1, complete picot, ch 5, s c in next loop of half motif, ch 5, skip 1 loop, s c in next loop, ch 1, sl st in corresponding picot of motif, ch 1, complete picot, ch 5, skip 1 loop of half motif, s c in next loop, ch 5, tr c cluster st in next s c, ch 1, sl st in corresponding picot of motif, ch 1, complete picot, ch 5, s c in next cluster st of half motif, ch 7, tr c cluster st in next loop, ch 1, sl st in corner picot of motif, ch 1, complete picot, ch 7, s c in next cluster st of half motif, ch 5, tr c cluster st in next s c, ch 3, sl st in top of cluster st for picot, ch 5, s c in next loop, ch 5, skip 1 loop, s c in next loop, ch 3, sl st in s c for picot, ch 5, skip 1 loop, s c in next loop, ch 5, tr c cluster st in next s c, ch 3, sl st in top of cluster st for picot, ch 5, s c in next cluster st, ch 7, tr c cluster st in next loop, ch 3, sl st in top of cluster st for picot, ch 7, s c in next cluster st, break thread. Join all half motifs in same manner following chart.

CROCHETED RUFFLE FOR TOP OF SPREAD: Ch 3, 2 d c in 3rd st from hook (shell) , ch 3, turn.

2nd Row. 2 d c in 1st d c, sl st in end ch.

3rd Row. Ch 3, turn, 2 d c in sl st, sl st in end ch. Repeat 3rd row until piece measures about 88 inches or length of spread.

Next Row. Ch 7, turn and working along side of shells, s c between next 2 shells, * ch 7, s c between next 2 shells, ch 7, s c in same space, ch 7, s c between next 2 shells, repeat from * for entire length, ch 1, turn.

Next Row. Sl st into loop, * ch 7, s c in next loop, repeat from * across row, ch 1, turn.

Next Row. Sl st into loop and work a tr c cluster st in same space, * ch 4, sl st in 3rd st from hook for picot, ch 1, tr c cluster st in same space, ch 4, s c in next loop, ch 4, tr c cluster st in next loop, repeat from * across row ending row to correspond, break thread.

Attach thread on opposite side and work in same manner. Work another ruffle in same manner.

EDGE FOR RUFFLE: With wrong side of work toward you, attach thread at beginning of ruffle, * ch 7, skip about ¼ inch space, s c in next space, repeat from * to end of ruffle, ch 1, turn.

Next Row. Repeat last row of crocheted ruffle. Work edge on all ruffles of spread and sham.

SHAM: Crochet a ruffle for sham same as crocheted ruffle for top of spread about 80 inches long.

FINISHING: Block motifs, sew to top of spread with "STAR" sewing thread as illustrated. Starch crocheted ruffles lightly, when dry press and sew to top of spread about 3½ inches in from side seam. Sew starched ruffle to sham about 2 inches in from heading of ruffle.

More Than a Touch of Blarney

MATERIALS:

CLARK'S O.N.T. MERCERIZED BEDSPREAD COTTON, White or
Ecru.

Single Size: 35 balls. **Double Size:** 43 balls.

Steel Crochet Hook No. 8.

GAUGE: Each block measures about 6 inches square. For single
size spread about 70 x 106 inches, including fringe, make 11 x 17
blocks. For double size spread about 88 x 106 inches, including
fringe, make 14 x 17 blocks.

BLOCK ... Ch 8. Join with sl st to form ring. **1st rnd:** Ch 1, 16 sc in
ring. Join with sl st in 1st sc. **2nd rnd:** Ch 1, sc in same place as sl
st, * ch 3, skip 1 sc, sc in next sc. Repeat from * around, joining last
ch-3 with sl st in 1st sc. **3rd rnd:** Sl st in next sp, in each sp around
make sc, h dc, 3 dc, h dc and sc (8 petals). **4th rnd:** * Ch 5, sc
behind next sc on last loop rnd. Repeat from * around, ending with
ch 5. **5th rnd:** In each loop around make sc, h dc, dc, 4 tr, dc, h dc
and sc. **6th rnd:** * Ch 6, sc behind next sc on last loop rnd, ch 9, sl st
in 9th ch from hook, in this ch-9 loop make sc, h dc, 3 dc, 5 tr, 3 dc, h
dc and sc, sl st in sc at base of loop. Repeat from * around. **7th rnd:**
In each ch-6 loop make sc, h dc, dc, 5 tr, dc, h dc, and sc. Join with
sl st in 1st sc of 1st petal. **8th rnd:** Sl st in h dc and in dc, ch 1, sc in
same place as last sl st, * ch 4, sc in next st, ch 6, skip 3 tr, sc in next
st, ch 4, sc in next st, ch 6, sc in dc of next petal. Repeat from *
around, joining last ch-6 with sl st in 1st sc.

9th rnd: Sl st in 4 ch, in sc and in next ch, sc in ch-6 loop, ch 4, sc in same loop, * ch 6, in next ch-6 loop make sc, ch 4 and sc. Repeat from * around. Join. **10th rnd:** Sl st in 4 ch, in sc and in next 2 ch, ch 4, in same loop make 2 tr, ch 5 and 3 tr, * (ch 6, in next loop make sc, ch 4 and sc) 3 times; ch 6, in next loop make 3 tr, ch 5 and 3 tr. Repeat from * around. Join with sl st in top st of 1st ch-4. **11th rnd:** Ch 4, tr in next 2 tr, * in corner sp make 3 tr, ch 5 and 3 tr, tr in next 3 tr, ch 6, sc in next loop, (ch 6, in next loop make sc, ch 4 and sc) twice; ch 6, sc in next loop, ch 6, tr in next 3 tr. Repeat from * around. Join. **12th rnd:** Ch 4, tr in 5 tr, * in next loop make 3 tr, ch 5 and 3 tr, tr in 6 tr, 3 tr in next loop, ch 6, sc in next loop, ch 6, in next loop make sc, ch 4 and sc, ch 6, sc in next loop, ch 6, 3 tr in next loop, tr in next 6 tr. Repeat from * around. Join. 13th rnd: Ch 4, tr in 8 tr, * in next loop make 3 tr, ch 5 and 3 tr, tr in 12 tr, 3 tr in next loop, (ch 3, tr in next loop) twice; ch 3, 3 tr in next loop, tr in next 12 tr. Repeat from * around. Join and fasten off.

Make necessary number of blocks and sew them together on wrong side with neat over and-over stitches, catching only one loop of each st on each edge. Attach thread to center st of a corner loop, ch 9, tr in same st, * ch 4, skip 3 sts, tr in next st. Repeat from * around one short and two long edges, making tr, ch 5 and tr at corners. Fasten off.

FRINGE . . . Make fringe in every other sp around one short and two long edges as follows: Cut 25 strands each 9 inches long. Double these strands, forming a loop. Pull loop through 1st sp and draw loose ends through loop. Pull tight. Trim evenly.

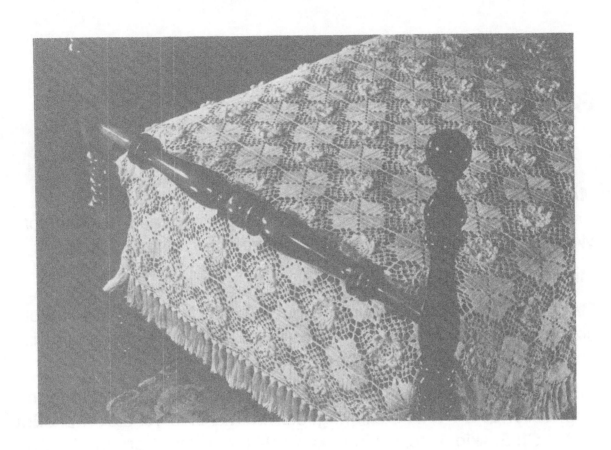

Beauty Rose Bedspread

MATERIALS...*Clark's O.N.T. Lustersheen, 55 skeins of White or Ecru, or 74 skeins of any color for double size spread; 46 skeins of White or Ecru, or 62 skeins of any color for single size spread.*

Milward's steel crochet hook No. 7.

GAUGE: Each block measures about 5 inches square. For a double size spread, 90 x 110 inches, make 18 x 22 blocks. For a single size spread, 75 x 110 inches, make 15 x 22 blocks.

FIRST BLOCK...Starting at center, ch 12 and join with sl st to form ring. **1st rnd:** Ch 1, 24 s c in ring. Join with sl st in 1st s c made. **2nd rnd:** * Ch 5, skip 3 s c, s c in next s c. Repeat from * around, ending with s c at base of ch-5 first made (6 loops). **3rd rnd:** In each ch-5 loop make: 1 s c, 1 half d c, 5 d c, 1 half d c, 1 s c (6 petals). **4th rnd:** Sl st in each st to center s c under 1st loop, * ch 5, s c in center s c under next loop. Repeat from * around, ending with sl st at base of ch-5 first made. **5th rnd:** In each ch-5 loop make: 1 s c, 1 half d c, 1 d c, 5 tr, 1 d c, 1 half d c, 1 s c. **6th rnd:** * Ch 7, skip 1 petal, s c in back of next s c of previous loop row. Repeat from * around. **7th rnd:** In each ch-7 loop make: 1 s c, 1 half d c, 1 d c, 7 tr, 1 d c, 1 half d c, 1 s c. **8th rnd:** Sl st to 1st tr of next petal, * ch 5, skip 5 tr, s c in next tr, ch 3, s c in same tr, ch 5, s c in 1st tr of next petal, ch 3, s c in same tr. Repeat from * around. **9th rnd:** Sl st in 1st loop, ch 4 (to count as tr), 2 tr in same loop, ** ch 3, 3 tr in same loop, * ch 5; in next loop make: s c, ch 3, s c. Repeat from * once more, ch 5, 3 tr in next ch-5 loop. Repeat from ** around, ending with ch 2, d c in 4th st of ch-4 first made. **10th rnd:** * Ch 5; s c, ch 3, s c in next loop. Repeat from * around. **11th rnd:** ** In next loop make: 1 s c, 1 half d c, 5 d c, 1 half d c, 1 s c (a shell made); s c in next ch-3 loop, in next ch-5 loop make another shell as before; * ch 5; s c, ch 3, s c in next

loop. Repeat from * once more, ch 5. Then repeat from ** around.
12th rnd: Sl st in each st to center d c of next shell, ** ch 5; in the s c between shells make: tr, ch 5, tr; ch 5, s c in center d c of next shell, * ch 5, s c, ch 3, s c in next loop. Repeat from * 2 more times, ch 5, s c in center d c of next shell.

Repeat from ** around. **13th rnd:** ** In each of next 3 loops make a shell as before; s c in next loop, ch 3, s c in same loop, * ch 5, s c, ch 3, s c in next loop. Repeat from * 2 more times. Then repeat from ** around. **14th rnd:** Sl st to center d c of next shell, ** ch 5, d c between this and next shell, ch 5; in 3rd d c of center shell make: tr, ch 5, tr; ch 5, d c between this and next shell, ch 5, s c in center d c of 3rd shell, * ch 5, s c, ch 3, s c in next loop. Repeat from * 2 more times, ch 5, s c in center d c of next shell. Repeat from ** around.
15th rnd: ** Make a shell in each of next 5 loops; s c, ch 3, s c in next loop; * ch 5, s c, ch 3, s c in next loop. Repeat from * 2 more times. Then repeat from ** around. Fasten and break off.

SECOND BLOCK...Work exactly as for first block to 14th rnd incl.
15th rnd: Make a shell in each of next 2 loops; in corner loop make: 1 s c, 1 half d c, 4 d c, s c in corresponding d c of corner shell of first block (always keeping right side of work on top), and complete shell on second block as before. * In next loop make: 1 s c, 1 half d c, 2 d c, s c in 3rd d c of corresponding shell on first block, and complete shell as before. Repeat from * once more. In next loop make s c, ch 3, s c; ** ch 2, s c in corresponding loop of first block, ch 2, s c in next loop back on second block, ch 3, s c in same loop. Repeat from ** 2 more times. *** In next ch-5 loop on second block make: 1 s c, 1 half d c, 2 d c, s c in 3rd d c of corresponding shell on first block, and complete shell as before. Repeat from *** once more. In corner loop make: 1 s c, 1 half d c, 1 d c, s c in corresponding d c of corner shell on first block, and complete shell. Finish remainder of rnd as for first block.

THIRD BLOCK...Work exactly as for second block, joining on last rnd to one side of first block (adjacent to side joined before).

FOURTH BLOCK... Work as for second block, joining on last rnd to one side of third block, and the adjacent side of second block.

Make necessary number of blocks, joining each block on the last rnd as before.

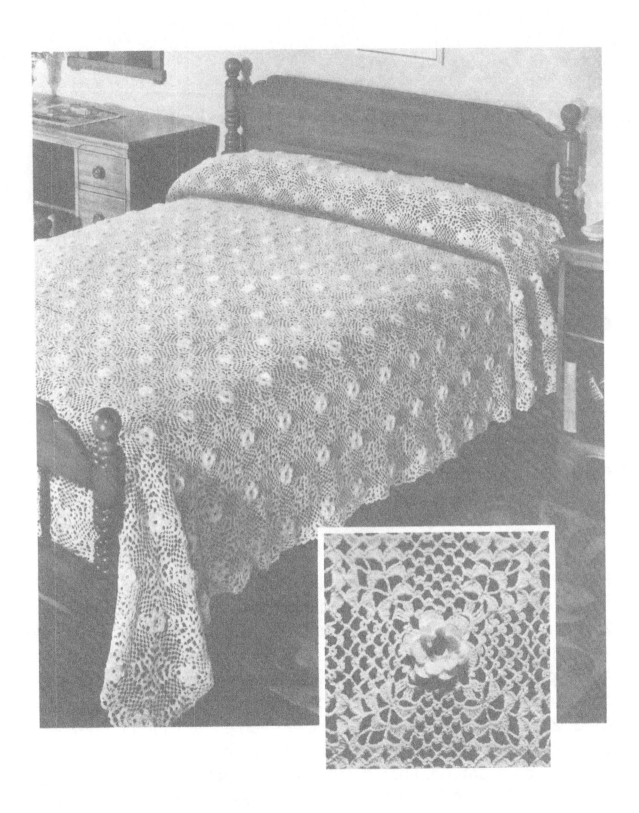

"Smilin' Through" Tablecloth

MATERIALS:

CLARK'S O.N.T. or J. & P. COATS BIG BALL BEST SIX CORD MERCERIZED CROCHET, size 30:

CLARK'S O.N.T.—33 balls of White or Ecru.

J. & P. COATS—33 balls of White or Ecru, or 44 balls of any color.

MILWARD'S Steel Crochet Hook No. 10 or 11.

GAUGE . . . Each motif measures 3½ inches from point to point, through center. For a tablecloth about 60 x 80 inches, make 17 x 23 motifs.

FIRST MOTIF . . . Starting at center, ch 9. **1st rnd:** In 9th ch from hook make d c, ch 5, d c, ch 5 and d c. Ch 2, d c in 4th st of ch-9. **2nd rnd:** Ch 3, 2 d c over bar of last d c, * d c in next st, 2 d c in next sp; in 3rd st of ch-5 make d c, ch 5 and d c (corner); 2 d c in same sp. Repeat from * around, ending with 2 d c in corner sp, d c where ch-3 started, ch 2, d c in 3rd st of ch-3 first made. **3rd and 4th rnds:** Ch 3, 2 d c over bar of last d c, * d c in each d c to within corner sp, 2 d c in sp. In 3rd st of corner ch-5 make d c, ch 5 and d c; 2 d c in sp. Repeat from * around, ending with 2 d c in last sp, d c where ch-3 started, ch 2, d c in 3rd st of ch-3 first made (19 d c between corner sps on 4th rnd). **5th rnd:** Ch 3, 2 d c over bar of d c, * d c in each of next 7 d c, ch 5, s c in 4th ch from hook (a p made). Ch 2, p, ch 2 (a double p-chain). Skip 5 d c, d c in next 7 d c, 2 d c in corner sp. In 3rd st of ch-5 make d c, ch 5 and d c; 2 d c in sp. Repeat from * around, ending with 2 d c in last sp, d c where ch-3 started, ch 2, d c in 3rd st of ch-3 first made.

6th rnd: Ch 3, 2 d c over bar of last d c, * d c in next 7 d c, a double p-chain, d c between 2 p's of p-chain below; make another double p-chain, skip 3 d c, d c in next 7 d c, 2 d c in sp. In 3rd st of corner ch-5 make d c, ch 5 and d c; 2 d c in sp. Repeat from * around, ending as before. **7th rnd:** Ch 3, 2 d c over bar of last d c, * d c in next 7 d c, a double p-chain, d c in d c, ch 1, p, ch 2 (a single p-chain) . D c in same place as last d c, a double p-chain, skip 3 d c, d c in next 7 d c, 2 d c in sp. In 3rd st of corner ch-5 make d c, ch 5 and d c; 2 d c in sp. Repeat from * around, ending as before. **8th rnd:** Ch 1, 2 s c in last d c, 2 s c over bar of same d c, * s c in next 7 d c, ch 1, p, ch 2, p, ch 2, p, ch 2 (a triple p-chain). D c in next d c; make a double p-chain, d c in next d c; make a triple p-chain, skip 3 d c, s c in next 7 d c, 2 s c in next sp, 3 s c in 3rd st of corner ch-5, 2 s c in sp. Repeat from * around, ending with 2 s c in last corner sp, sl st in ch-1 first made.

9th rnd: Ch 1, 3 s c in next s c, * s c in next 7 s c, a double p-chain, d c between 1st 2 p's of next triple p-chain; a double p-chain, d c in next d c, a single p-chain. D c between p's of next p-chain, a single p-chain, d c in next d c, a double p-chain, d c between last 2

p's of next triple p-chain. A double p-chain, skip 3 s c, s c in next 7 s c, 3 s c in next s c. Repeat from * around, ending with skip 3 s c, s c in next 7 s c. Sl st in ch-1 first made. **10th rnd:** Sl st to center s c of 3-s c group (corner), ch 1, 2 s c where ch-1 started, ** s c in next 5 s c, * a double p-chain, d c in next d c. Repeat from * 4 more times, a double p-chain, skip 3 s c, s c in each st to within corner s c, 3 s c in next s c. Repeat from ** around, ending with s c in last 5 sts, sl st in ch-1 first made. Fasten off. This completes one motif.

SECOND MOTIF . . . Work 1st 9 rnds as for first motif. **10th rnd:** Sl st to center of 3-s c group (corner), ch 1, 2 s c where ch-1 started, * s c in next 5 s c; (double p-chain, d c in next d c) 4 times; ch 1, p, ch 4, sl st in corresponding p of first motif, ch 1, s c in 3rd ch of ch-4, ch 1, d c in next d c on second motif. (Ch 4, sl st in next p of first motif, ch 1, s c in 3rd ch of last ch-4) twice. Ch 1, skip 3 s c, s c in next 5 s c, 2 s c in next s c , sl st in center of 3-s c group on first motif, ch 1. Continue as for first motif, joining next 3 p's as last 3 p's were joined. Make necessary number of motifs, joining as before (6 free p's on each motif between joinings).

FILL-IN LACE . . . Starting at center, ch 9. **1st rnd:** D c in 9th ch from hook; in same ch make ch 5, d c, ch 5 and d c; ch 5, sl st in 4th st of ch-9. **2nd rnd:** Ch 1, * in next sp make half d c, d c and 2 tr; ch 2, sl st in 3rd p to left of joining, ch 2, sl st in last tr made, 2 tr in same place as last tr, ch 2, sl st in next free p on motif, ch 2, sl st in last tr; tr, d c and half d c in same place as last tr; s c in next d c. Repeat from * 3 more times. Join and fasten off. Fill in all spaces in this manner. Block cloth to measurements given.

Tiny rosebuds join the crossed motifs of this filmy Irish lace cloth—there's a smart squared effect in this refreshing design.

73

A Tournament of Roses Spread

Linen and Irish Crochet, over a flash of color—a showy bedspread for a master bedroom . . . for the center of attention in any bedroom, Use the principal color of the room for the flounce.

MATERIALS—Lily Homestead Crochet and Knitting Cotton in Ecru (Art. 131 in skeins or Art. 205 in balls) :—SINGLE SIZE—(64" x 91") —14-skeins or 12-balls Ecru. DOUBLE SIZE—(76" x 91")—16—skeins or 14-balls Ecru. 4⅓-yds. off-white linen 36" wide for single size or 48" wide for double size. Crochet hook size 10.

BLOCK—(Size-4½"—Ch 7, sl st in 1st st. Ch 5, dc in ring, (ch 2, dc in ring) 6 times, ch 2, sl st in 3d st of 1st 5-ch. ROW 2—(Ch 1, 3 dc in next sp, ch 1, sc in next dc) 8 times, ending with sl st instead of sc. ROW 3—(Ch 4, sc behind petal into back lp of sc between petals) 8 times, ending with sl st instead of sc. ROW 4—(Ch 1, 5 dc in next lp, ch 1, sc in next sc) 8 times, ending with sl st. ROW 5——(Ch 6, sc in back lp of next sc between petals) 8 times, ending with sl st. ROW 6 —Like Row 4 but with 8 dc petals. ROW 7—Like Row 5 but with 7-ch lps. ROW 8—* Ch 2, dc in next lp, (ch 2, tr) 3 times in same lp, ch 2, dc in same lp, ch 2, sc in next sc. Repeat from * 7 times, ending with sl st. ROW 9—* 2 sc in next sp, (3 sc in next sp) 4 times, 2 sc in next sp. Repeat from * 7 times. ROW 10—Sl st in 1st 6 sc, (ch 13, sc in next 5th sc, ch 13, sc in 6th sc on next petal) 8 times. ROW 11—Ch 5, * dc in one lp of 7th (center) st of next lp, (ch 2, dc) 4 times in same st, tr in sc between lps. Repeat from * around. Sl st in top of 1st 5-ch. Cut 6" long, thread to a needle and fasten off on back.

2d BLOCK—Join the 1st 3 shells in Row 11 to the 1st 3 shells on 1st Block, as follows:—Work 1st shell thru to 3d (center) dc, ch 4, sl st in center dc of 3d shell on 1st Block, ch 4 back, sl st in last dc and complete shell. Join 2d shell on each Block in same way but with 2-ch lps. Join 3d shell to 1st shell on 1st Block in same way, with 4-ch lps. Complete Block. Continue to make and join Blocks by 3 shells on each side of each, leaving one shell free between joining of Blocks. Always start joinings by the 1st 3 shells in Row 11.

FILL-IN MOTIF—(Between every 4 Blocks)—Ch 6, sl st in 1st st. Ch 1, 8 sc in ring, sl st in 1st sc. Ch 8, sl st in a free shell on one Block, * ch 8, sc back in next sc on ring, ch 12, sl st in 4-ch joining of Blocks, ch 12, sc back in next sc on ring. Repeat from * 3 times. Fasten off.

CENTER—For single size spread, make 84 Blocks and join 6 x 14. For double size make 112 Blocks and join 8 x 14. EDGE—Join to 1st free shell on a corner Block, ch 3 for a dc, (ch 11, dc in next shell) 8 times, * ch 7, dc in 4-ch between Blocks, ch 7, dc in next shell, (ch 11, dc in next shell) 4 times. Repeat from * around, with each corner like 1st one. Join final 7-ch to 3d st of 1st 14-ch. ROW 2—Ch 3, (11 dc in next lp, 1 dc in de) 8 times, * 5 dc in next lp, (1 dc in same lp, 1 dc in dc in angle and 1 dc in next 7-ch lp) holding back the last lp of each dc on hook, thread over and pull thru all 4 lps at once for a Cluster, 5 dc in bal. of same 7-ch lp, 1 dc in next dc, (11 dc in next sp, 1 dc in next dc) 4 times. Repeat from * around with each corner like 1st one. Join and fasten off.

1st BORDER ROW—Following Chart, make and join 17 Blocks into a straight row for one side of bed. Repeat for other side. Then join these 2 rows with 7 Blocks for single size or 9 Blocks for double size, —across bottom of spread. Repeat 2 rows of "Edge" around all sides of this Border Row.

2d BORDER ROW—Make a row of 17 Blocks for each side of spread. Make a row of 9 Blocks for bottom edge of single size or 11 Blocks for double size. Repeat "Edge" around each of these pieces.

PILLOW—Make 24 Blocks and join 4 x 6. Repeat "Edge" around this piece. Stretch and pin each section right-side-down in true matching shapes. Steam and press dry thru a cloth.

Cut a length of linen (full width) 78" long. Pin 1st Border Row around 2 sides and one end of this piece. Then pin "Center" in center of linen with the same distance between it and Border at bottom as on sides. The Blocks in "Center" should line up *between* the Blocks in Border Row (as in Chart). Split remaining linen lengthwise into 3 equal strips.

Pin a strip under outside edge of each side of 1st Border Row. Pin one piece of 2d Border Row on outside edge of each strip (see Chart, p. 27). The Blocks in both Border Rows should line up exactly.

Baste Edge of Blocks down on linen, then whip the edge down closely. Working on wrong side, cut linen out underneath Blocks ¼" inside stitching. Turn this edge back against crochet and hem down on back of dc-row.

Stretch finished spread right-side-down on curtain or quilting frames and block.

Make an under-spread of sateen, broadcloth or glazed chintz in desired color, finishing edge with a flounce to reach to floor. Make a case for pillow of same material, finishing it with a ruffle cut 8" wide and folded lengthwise thru center. Miter corners. Tack Pillow Section over this pillow case.

Irish Lace Tablecloth

ROYAL SOCIETY SIX CORD CORDICHET, Size 50: 45 balls of White or Ecru. Steel Crochet Hook No. 12. Cloth measures about 72 inches square.

GAUGE: Each motif measures about 5 inches square.

FIRST MOTIF . . . Starting at center, ch 6. Join with sl st to form ring. **1st rnd:** Ch 1; 12 sc in ring. Join with sl st in 1st sc. **2nd rnd:** Ch 3, dc in same place as sl st, 2 dc in each sc around. Join with sl st in top st of starting chain (24 dc, counting starting chain as 1 dc). **3rd rnd**: Ch 1, sc in same place as sl st, * ch 7, skip next dc, sc in next dc, (ch 5, skip next dc, sc in next dc) twice. Repeat from * 3 more times, joining last ch-5 with sl st in 1st sc of rnd. 4th rnd: Sl st to center st of next ch-7 loop, ch 1, sc in same loop, * ch 7, sc in same loop, (ch 5, sc in next loop) 3 times. Repeat from * around. Join. 5th rnd: Sl st to center st of next ch-7 loop, ch 1, sc in same loop, * ch 7, sc in same loop, (ch 5, sc in next loop) 4 times. Repeat from * around. Join. **6th rnd:** Sl st to center st of next loop, ch 1, sc in same loop, * ch 7, sc in same loop, ch 5, sc in next loop, ch 8, make a 5-d tr cluster in center st of next loop—*to make a 5-d tr cluster, holding back on hook the last loop of each d tr, make 5 d tr in same place, thread over and draw through all loops on hook;* make a cluster in center st of next loop, ch 8, sc in next loop, ch 5, sc in next loop. Repeat from * around. Join. **7th rnd:** Sl st to center st of next loop, ch 1, sc in same loop, * ch 7, sc in same loop, ch 5, sc in next loop, ch 5, sl st in 4th st of ch-8; make a cluster of 3 (instead of 5) d tr in the st between clusters of last rnd, ch 7, sl st in same place as last cluster, ch 7, make a 3-d tr cluster in the same place, sl st in 5th st of next ch-8, (ch 5, sc in next loop) twice. Repeat from * around. Join.

8th rnd: Sl st to center st of next loop, ch 1, sc in same loop, * ch 7, sc in same loop, (ch 5, sc in next loop) twice; ch 5, in center of previous clusters make a 5-d tr cluster, ch 5, and a 5-d tr cluster; (ch 5, sc in next loop) 3 times. Repeat from * around. Join. **9th rnd:** Sl st to center st of next loop, ch 1, sc in same loop, * ch 7, sc in same loop, (ch 5, sc in next loop) 4 times; ch 5, sc in same loop, (ch 5, sc in next loop) 4 times. Repeat from * around,. Join. **10th rnd:** Sl st to center st of next loop, ch 1, sc in same loop, * ch 7, sc in same loop, ch 5, sc in next loop, ch 8, (make a 5-d tr cluster in center st of next loop) twice; ch 8, sc in next loop, (ch 5, sc in next loop) twice; ch 8, (make a 5-d tr cluster in center st of next loop) twice; ch 8, sc in next loop, ch 5. sc in next loop. Repeat from * around. Join. 11th rnd: Sl st to center st of next loop, ch 1, sc in same loop, ** ch 7, sc in same loop, ch 5, sc in next loop, * ch 5. sl st in 4th st of ch-8; between clusters of last rnd make a 3-d tr cluster, ch 7, sl st in same place, ch 7, and a 3-d tr cluster; sl st in 5th st of next ch-8; (ch 5. sc in next loop) twice. Repeat from * once more; then repeat from ** around. Join. 12th rnd: Sl st to center st of next loop, ch 1, sc in same loop, ** ch 9, sc in same loop, (ch 7, sc in next loop) twice; * ch 7, in center of previous clusters make a 5-d tr cluster, ch 5 and a 5-d tr cluster; (ch 7, sc in next loop) 3 times. Repeat from * once more; then repeat from ** around. Join. 13th rnd: Sl st to center st of next loop, ch 1, sc in same loop,

** ch 9, sc in same loop, * (ch 7, sc in next loop) 3 times; ch 5, sc in same loop, (ch 5, sc in next loop) twice; ch 5, sc in same loop. Repeat from * once more; (ch 7, sc in next sp) 3 times. Repeat from ** around. Join and break off.

SECOND MOTIF . . . Work same as First Motif until 12th rnd is completed. 13th rnd: Sl st to center st of next loop, ch 1, sc in same loop, ch 4, sc in corner of First Motif, ch 4, sc in same loop on Second Motif, * (ch 3, sc in next loop on First Motif, ch 3, sc in next loop on Second Motif) 3 times; ch 2, sc in next loop on First Motif, ch 2, sc in same loop on Second Motif, (ch 2, sc in next loop on First Motif, ch 2, sc in next loop on Second Motif) twice; ch 2, sc in next loop on First Motif, ch 2, sc in same loop on Second Motif. Repeat from * once more; (ch 3, sc in next loop on First Motif, ch 3, sc in next loop on Second Motif) 3 times; ch 4, sc in corner loop on First Motif, ch 4, sc in same loop on Second Motif. Complete 13th rnd same as 13th rnd of First Motif (no more joinings).

Make 15 x 15 Motifs, joining adjacent sides as Second Motif was joined to First Motif (where 4 corners meet join 3rd and 4th corners to joinings of previous two).

EDGING . . . Attach thread in a corner loop, ch 1, sc in same loop, ** ch 7, sl st in 4th ch from hook, ch 3, sc in same loop, * ch 7, sl st in 4th ch from hook, ch 3, sc in next loop. Repeat from * across to next corner loop. Repeat from ** around. Join and break off. Block to measurements given.

Wedding Ring Bedspread

Approximate Size: 82 inches by 105 inches **MATERIALS: Bucilla Wondersheen Crochet and Knitting**

Cotton, Article 3666, 23 skeins; or

Bucilla Blue Label Super Crochet and Knitting Cotton,

Article 3457 22 skeins,

1 **Bucilla Steel Crochet Hook, No. 9, Article 4300.**

Gauge: Each oval should measure 5 inches from point to point. Each square should measure 2 and ⅞ inches.

Ovals—Ch 39, work 1 s c in 9th st from hook, * ch 5, skip 2 sts on chain, work 1 s c in next st; repeat from * 9 times, then ch 5, work another s c in same place as last s c; work along other side of foundation chain by working ch 5 and 1 s c in the st directly opposite the s c on first side of foundation chain, end with ch 5, 1 s c in 3rd st of first loop of round, ch 3, work 1 d c in same place as the last s c was worked in (11 loops on each side of foundation chain, with a point loop at each end of chain). *2nd round:* ch 5 and 1 s c in each of 11 spaces to point, ch 5, 1 s c in point space, ch 5, 1 more s c in same space, ch 5 and 1 s c in each of the next 11 spaces, ch 5, 1 s c in point space, ch 3, 1 d c in same space. *3rd round:* ch 5 and 1 s c in each space to point space, ch 5, 1 s c in point space, ch 5, 1 more s c in point space, ch 5 and 1 s c in each space to other point space, end same as round below. *4th round:* same as 3rd round, but ending round with 1 s c in point space. *5th round:* ch 4 and 1 s c in each space of round, join with ch 4 and 1 s c in the point space of round below and fasten off thread (there will be 15 spaces on each side of oval). Make 520 of these oval motifs.

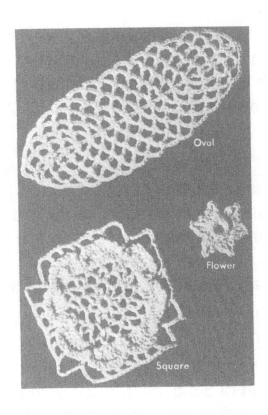

Oval

Flower

Square

Squares—Ch 7, join with a slip st into a ring. *1st round:* ch 4, work 1 s c in ring, * ch 4 and 1 s c in same ring; repeat from * 5 times, then ch 3, work 1 d c in ring (8 loops in ring, including the loop formed by ch 3 and 1 d c). *2nd round:* ch 4 and 1 s c in each space of round below to within 1 space of end of round, ch 2, 1 d c in last space (8 spaces in round). *3rd round:* * ch 4, work 1 s c in next space, ch 4, 1 more s c in same space; repeat from * around, end with ch 4, 1 s c in last space, ch 3, 1 d c in same space. *4th round:* ch 3 and 1 s c in each space of round below. *5th round:* * 2 d c in next space, 3 trebles (twice over hook) in same space, then 3 trebles in next space, 2 d c in same space, 1 s c in next s c; repeat from * around, join with a slip st in first s c of round (8 petals in round). *6th round:* ch 3, turn, work 1 slip st in back thread of first st, ch 3 and 1 slip st in back thread of each st of round. *7th round:* ch 11, turn, skip first 3 sts on first petal, * work 1 treble on free thread of next st (directly in back of the frill edge), ch 2, skip 1 st, 1 treble on free thread of next st, ch 2, skip next st, 1 treble on free thread of next st, skip the next 5 sts, work 1 treble on free thread of next st, ch 2, skip 1 st, 1 treble on free thread of next st, ch 2, skip next st, 1 treble on

85

free thread of next st, ch 8, 1 d c on free thread of the s c worked between next 2 petals, ch 8, skip the next 3 sts; repeat from * around, end with ch 8, join with a slip st in 3rd st of ch 11 at beginning of round and fasten off thread. Make 238 of these square motifs.

Flowers—Ch 7, join with a slip st into a ring, work 12 s c in ring, 1 slip st on front thread of each st of round below, join with a slip st on *back* thread of 1st st of round. *Petals:* * ch 2, 1 d c on free thread of next s c, ch 3, 1 more d c in same st, ch 2, 1 s c on free thread of next st; repeat from * around, join with a slip st in first slip st at beginning of round and fasten off. Make 757 of these flowers.

Joining—*Lower Half of 1st row:* (A on chart) working from right side of work make 3 s c in first space after point s c on an oval motif, ch 3, work 1 slip st in top of last s c (picot), 2 more s c in same space, * work a group of 3 s c, ch 3, picot, 2 more s c, —all in next space; repeat from * until there are 15 picots completed from beginning, ending with 2 s c after last picot in space just before point, * ch 5, pick up a new oval motif and work in same way along the side of this motif, ch 5, pick up a 3rd oval motif and work 2 s c in first space, after point, ch 2, drop loop from hook, insert it in last picot made on 2nd oval motif, also insert hook in the dropped loop and draw through, ch 1, complete the picot, work 2 more s c in same space on new motif, 3 s c in next space, ch 2, drop loop from hook, insert it in the next picot on 2nd motif, also insert it in the dropped loop and draw through, ch 1, complete the picot, 2 s c in same space on new motif, 3 s c, ch 3, picot, 2 more s c,—all in next space, 2 s c in next space, ch 6, work a slip st in 4th st from hook, ch 6, a slip st in 4th st from hook, ch 2, drop loop from hook, skip 1 picot, on 2nd motif, insert hook in next picot, also insert it in the dropped loop and draw through, ch 6, picot, ch 6, picot, ch 2, slip st in top of last s c on 3rd motif 2 more s c in same space (a 4-picot joining), continue in picot edging to point of motif, then repeat from * until there are 20 oval motifs joined into a row.

Upper half of 1st row: continue to work picot edging along other half of 20th motif to connecting chain, work 7 s c under this chain, then work 3 s c in next space on 19th oval motif, ch 2, join to picot on 20th motif, ch 1, finish picot, 2 s c in same space on 19th motif, 3 s c in next space, ch 2, join to next picot on 20th motif, ch 1, complete the picot, 2 more s c in same space on 19th motif, work picot edging in next space, 3 s c in next space, skip 1 picot on 20th motif, join with a 4-picot joining to next free picot on 20th motif, continue in picot edging in each of the next 6 spaces on 19th motif, work 3 s c in next space, ch 3, pick up a square motif and work 4 s c under a ch 8 after the d c, 4 s c in each of the next 2 spaces on new motif, skip 2 picots on 19th oval motif, join with a picot to next free picot on oval motif, then work 4 s c in each of the next 3 spaces on square motif, skip 2 picots on oval motif, join with a picot to next picot on oval motif, 8 s c in same corner space, 8 s c in next corner space, join with a picot to first free picot on 20th oval motif, 4 more s c in same space. In same way as before, join 2 more picots of square to 2 picots on 20th oval motif, work 8 s c in same corner space on square as the last joining picot, 8 s c in next space, ch 3, picot, 4 more s c in same space, 4 s c in each of the next 2 spaces, ch 3, picot, 4 s c in each of the next 3 spaces, ch 3, picot, 8 more s c in same corner space, continue in this way along 4th side of square, ending with 8 s c in same space as the 4 s c at beginning of round, join with a slip st in first s c of round, ch 1, 1 slip st under the connecting chain, ch 1, slip st in last s c made on 19th oval motif, 2 more s c in same space as last used on 19th motif, continue in picot edging along upper edge of oval motif, 7 s c under connecting chain, then repeat from beginning of row to end, thus joining in the squares in places as shown on chart (see page 30), join with a slip st in first s c of lower half of 1st row.

Chart for Wedding Ring Bedspread

Lower half of 2nd row: ch 5, pick up a new oval motif, work 3 s c in first space after point, join with a picot to last picot made in last row, continue joining as in row below, with a picot in next picot in 1st row, leave 1 picot free, then join with a 4-picot joining to next picot of 1st oval motif of 1st row; join with picots in same way as before, 3 picots on one side of square to the corresponding picots in oval motif, work in picot edging along lower edge of oval motif to point, join another oval motif in same way as before, to first 4 picots of last oval motif, then join to the next 3 picots on square motif as before, join to the last 4 picots on 2nd motif of 1st row; ch 5, pick up a new oval motif and join the first 4 picots on 3rd motif of 1st row as before to 4 picots of new oval, join the next 3 picots of next square motif in same way as before to the new oval motif; continue in this way to join motif after motif until there are 20 oval motifs joined in this row, ending with 2 s c in space just before point st, ch 5, join to point st of 20th motif of first row, work 7 s c under this chain. Work in picot edging along upper edge of 1st oval motif, then continue along this side of row in same way as upper half of 1st row. Continue in this way to join motifs in places as shown in illustration, diagram and detail cut until all motifs are joined, then work down the free side of spread in same way, join at end of round.

Edging—Slip st to center of first picot of first oval motif of 1st row, work ch 5 and 1 s c in each of the next 14 picots, * ch 5, 1 s c under next chain (the connecting chain between motifs), ch 5 and 1 s c in each of the next 24 picots; repeat from * to corner of spread, work this corner like first, then continue around, working all corners alike, join with a slip st in first st of round. *2nd round:* turn, slip st to center of first space, 1 s c in space, * ch 5, 1 more s c in same space, ch 5, 1 s c in next space, ch 5, 1 more s c in same space, ch 5 and 1 s c in each of the next 10 spaces, ch 5, skip 1 space, 1 s c in next space, ch 5, skip next space, 1 s c in next space, ch 5 and 1 s c in each of the next 10 spaces; repeat from * to corner motif of spread, ch 5, 1 s c, ch 5, all in space before joining of motifs, 1 s c in next space, ch 5, 1 more s c in same space, ch 5 and 1 s c in each space to next joining of motifs, work in these 2 spaces in same way as other 2 joining spaces, then continue around, as before, working all corners alike, join with ch 5 and a slip st in first s c of round. *3rd round:* turn, slip st in each st of first space, then slip st to center of next space, work 1 s c in space, † * ch 5 and 1 s c in next space, ch 6, picot, ch 6, picot, ch 2, skip 1 space, 1 s c in next space (a 2-picot loop) ; repeat from * 3 times, then ch 5, 1 s c in next space, work a 2-picot loop in next space, ch 5 and 1 s c in each of the next 2 spaces, work a 2-picot loop in next space, * ch 5, 1 s c in next space, skip next space, work a 2-picot loop in next space; repeat from last * twice, omit the chain after last s c, work 1 s c in next space, ch 5, 1 s c in next space, 1 s c in next space, skip next space, work a 2-picot loop in next space, ch 5 and 1 s c in next space, skip next space, a 2-picot loop in next space, ch 5 and 1 s c in next space, skip next space, a 2-picot loop in next space; repeat from † to corner motif of spread, work along the side of this motif as before, then work a 2-picot loop in the increased loop of round below, ch 5, and 1 s c in each of the next 2 spaces, skip next space, work a 2-picot loop in next space, continue in this way around entire spread, working all corners alike,—join with a slip st in first s c of round, slip st to center of next space. *Final round:* 1 s c in space, ch 6, picot, ch 6, a 2nd picot, ch 6, a 3rd picot, ch 2, skip the picot loop below, work 1 s c in next space (a 3-picot loop) work a 3-picot loop over each 2-picot loop below, then work ch 6, picot, ch 2, over the plain loops, continue in this way around entire spread, join with a slip st in first s c of round and fasten off thread. Tack the small flower motifs in places as shown in diagram (see page 30), and illustration tacking each petal in place.

Irish Rose Ruffle

Materials Required: AMERICAN THREAD COMPANY "STAR" MERCERIZED CROCHET COTTON, ARTICLE 30 Size 50

4—125 yd. Balls White.

Steel Crochet Hook No. 13.

Doily measures about 10½ inches without ruffle.

Ch 6, join to form a ring, ch 6, d c in ring, * ch 3, d c in ring, repeat from * 3 times, ch 3, join in 3rd st of ch.

2nd Row. Ch 1, * 2 d c, 5 tr c, 2 d c in mesh, s c in next d c, repeat from * all around.

3rd Row. * Ch 6, s c in next s c in back of petal, repeat from * all around.

4th Row. In each loop work 2 d c, 7 tr c, 2 d c and l s c in s c between petals.

5th Row. Ch 10, sl st in 5th st from hook for picot, ch 7, sl st in 5th st from hook for picot, ch 2, s c in center st of next petal, ** ch 7, sl st in 5th st from hook for picot, ch 7, sl st in 5th st from hook for picot, ch 2, d c between petals, * ch 7, sl st in 5th st from hook for picot, repeat from *, ch 2, s c in center st of next petal, repeat from ** 4 times, * ch 7, sl st in 5th st from hook for picot, repeat from *, ch 2, join in 3rd st of ch.

6th Row. * Ch 7, s c between picots of next loop, ch 7, s c in next s c, ch 7, s c between picots of next loop, ch 7, s c in next d c, repeat from * all around.

7th Row. Sl st to center of next loop, ch 8, d c in same loop, * ch 2, 1 d c, ch 5, l d c in next loop, repeat from * all around ending row with ch 2, join in 3rd st of ch.

8th Row. Sl st to center of next loop, ch 5, s c in same loop, * ch 2, skip the ch 2 loop, 3 d c in next loop, ch 5, sl st in top of last d c for picot, 5 d c in same loop, ch 5, sl st in top of last d c for picot, 3 d c in same loop, (shell) ch 2, skip the next 2 ch loop. 1 s c, ch 5, 1 s c in next loop, repeat from * all around ending row with ch 2, skip the 2 ch loop, 3 d c, picot, 5 d c, picot, 3 d c in next loop, ch 2, join.

9th Row. Sl st into 5 ch loop, ch 7, s c in center d c of next shell, ch 5, s c in same space, ch 7, * s c in next 5 ch loop, ch 7, s c in center d c of next shell, ch 5, s c in same space, ch 7, repeat from * all around.

10th Row. Sl st to center of next loop, ch 8, d c in same space, ch 7, sl st in 5th st from hook for picot, ch 2, 1 d c, ch 5, 1 d c in center st of next ch 7 loop, repeat from * all around ending row with ch 7, sl st in 5th st from hook for picot, ch 2, join in 3rd st of ch.

11th Row. Sl st into loop, * ch 5, s c in same space, ch 9. skip the picot loop, s c in next loop, repeat from * all around ending row with ch 4, tr c in sl st, (this brings thread in position for next row) .

12th Row. Ch 8, d c in same space, ch 5, d c in same space, * ch 7, sl st in 5th st from hook for picot, ch 2, I d c, ch 5. I d c in center st of next 9 ch loop, ch 7, sl st in 5th st from hook for picot, ch 2, d c in center st of next 9 ch loop, ch 5, d c in same space, ch 5, d c in same space, repeat from * all around ending row with ch 7, sl st in 5th st from hook for picot, ch 2, 1 d c, ch 5, 1 d c in next 9 ch loop, ch 7, sl st in 5th st from hook for picot, ch 2, join in 3rd st of ch.

13th Row. Sl st to loop, * ch 7, s c in next loop, ch 7, skip the picot loop, 1 s c, ch 5, 1 s c in next loop, ch 7, skip the picot loop, s c in next loop, repeat from * all around.

Next 4 Rows. Repeat 10th, 11th, 12th and 13th rows.

18th Row. Sl st into loop, ch 3 (counts as 1 d c) 2 d c, picot, 5 d c, picot, 3 d c (shell) in same loop, * ch 2, 1 d c, ch 5, 1 d c in center st of next loop, ch 7, sl st in 5th st from hook for picot, ch 2, 1 d c, ch 5, 1 d c in center st of next 7 ch loop, ch 2, 3 d c, picot, 5 d c, picot, 3 d c in next loop, repeat from * all around ending row with ch 2, 1 d c, ch 5, 1 d c in center st of next loop, ch 7, sl st in 5th st from hook for picot, ch 2, 1 d c, ch 5, I d c in center st of next loop, ch 2, join.

19th Row. Sl st to center of shell, * ch 5, s c in same space, ch 7, s c in next 5 ch loop, ch 5, s c in same space, ch 7, skip the picot loop, 1 s c, ch 5, 1 s c in next loop, ch 7, 1 s c in center d c of next shell, repeat from * all around ending row with ch 5, s c in same space, ch 7, s c in next 5 ch loop, ch 5, s c in same space, ch 7, skip the picot loop, s c in next 5 ch loop, ch 5, s c same space, ch 7, join. Repeat 10th, 11th, 12th and 13th rows once, then repeat 10th and 11th rows.

26th Row. S c in loop, * ch 10, s c in next ch 9 loop, repeat from * all around ending row with ch 5, d tr c (3 times over needle) in s c.

27th Row. S c in loop, * ch 10, s c in next loop, repeat from * all around ending row with ch 5, d tr c in s c.

RUFFLE: Sl st into loop, * ch 10, s c in same loop, repeat from * twice, ** ch 10, s c in next loop, * ch 10, s c in same loop, repeat from * twice, repeat from ** all around ending row with ch 5, d tr c in sl st.

2nd Row. * Ch 10, s c in next loop, repeat from * all around ending row with ch 5, d tr c in d tr c. Repeat last row 5 times.

8th Row. Ch 1, s c in same space, * ch 5, sl st in top of s c for picot, ch 8, 3 d c, picot, 5 d c, picot, 3 d c in next loop, ch 8, s c in next loop, repeat from * all around, break thread.

Irish Rose Edging

For	AMERICAN THREAD CO. Materials Required	Needle
Luncheon Mats or Sheets and Cases	STAR Tatting Cotton Article 25.........	13
Tablecloths	STAR Crochet Cotton Article 20 or 30, Size 30 or......................	1ı
	GEM Crochet Cotton Article 35, Size 30..	11
Towels	DELUXE Knitting and Crochet Cotton Article 346 or....................	7
	PURITAN Cotton Article 40 or...........	7
	STAR Pearl Cotton Article 90...........	7

Shaded Pinks and White or Colors Desired

With Shaded Pinks ch 5, join to form a ring, ch 6, d c in ring, * ch 3, d c in ring, repeat from * 3 times, ch 3, join in 3rd st of ch.

2nd Row. Over each loop, work l s c, l s d c, 3 d c, l s d c, 1 s c (s d c: thread over hook, insert in space, pull through, thread over and pull through all loops at one time). 3rd Row. * Ch 5, s c in back of work between the s c of next 2 petals, repeat from * all around.

4th Row. Over each loop, work 1 s c, 1 s d c, 5 d c, 1 s d c, l s c.

5th Row. * Ch 7, s c in back of work between next 2 petals, repeat from * all around.

6th Row. Over each loop, work 1 s c, 1 d c, 7 tr c, 1 d c, l s c, join, break thread.

Attach White in center of any petal, * ch 7, thread over hook, insert in last tr c of same petal, pull through, thread over and work off 2 loops, thread over hook, insert in 1st tr c of next petal, pull through, thread over and work off 2 loops, thread over and pull through all loops at one time, ch 7, s c in center st of same petal, repeat from * all around, join.

2nd Row. Sl st into loop, ch 3, 2 d c in same space keeping last loop of each d c on hook, thread over and pull through all loops at one time, ch 9, cluster st in same space (cluster st: thread over hook, insert in space, pull through and work off 2 loops, * thread over hook, insert in same space, pull through and work off 2 loops, repeat from * once, thread over and pull through all loops at one time) , * ch 7, s c in next loop, ch 3, s c in same space, ch 7, s c in next loop, ch 3, s c in same space, ch 7, 2 cluster sts with ch 9 between in next loop (corner), repeat from * all around ending row with * ch 7, s c in next loop, ch 3, s c in same space, repeat from * once, ch 7, join. Work a 2nd flower joining it to 1st flower in last row as follows: sl st into loop, ch 3, 2 d c in same space keeping last loop of each d c on hook, thread over and pull through all loops at one time, ch 4, join to corner loop of 1st flower, ch 4, cluster st in same loop of 2nd flower, * ch 3, s c in next loop of 1st flower, ch 3, s c in next loop of 2nd flower, ch 3, s c in same space, repeat from * once, ch 3, s c in next loop of 1st flower, ch 3, cluster st in next loop of 2nd flower, ch 4, join to next corner loop of 1st flower, ch 4, cluster st in same loop of 2nd flower and complete row same as 1st flower. Join all flowers in same manner.

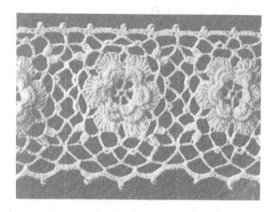

Heading. Attach White at corner loop of 1st flower, ch 10, 2 s c in next ch 7 loop, * ch 7, 2 s c in next ch 7 loop, ch 7, 2 s c in next ch 9 loop, ch 5, d c in joining, ch 5, 2 s c in next ch 7 loop, repeat from * across row, break thread. Attach thread in 3rd st of ch and work ** 4 s c in next loop, s c in next s c, ch 4, sl st in top of last s c for picot, s c in next s c, * 6 s c in next loop, s c in next s c, picot, s c in next s c, repeat from * once, 4 s c in next loop, s c in next d c, ch 4, sl st in top of last s c for picot, repeat from ** across row, break thread.

Lower Edge. Attach White in corner loop of 1st flower, * ch 8, s c in next ch 7 loop, ch 8, s c in next ch 7 loop, ch 8, s c in next ch 7 loop, ch 8, s c in joining, repeat from * across row, ch 8, turn.

Next Row. S c in next loop, * ch 8, s c in next loop, repeat from * twice, * ch 4, s c in next loop, * ch 8, s c in next loop, repeat from * twice, repeat from ** across row, ch 1, turn.

Next Row. 5 s c, 4 ch picot, 5 s c over each ch 8 loop and 5 s c over each ch 4 loop, break thread.

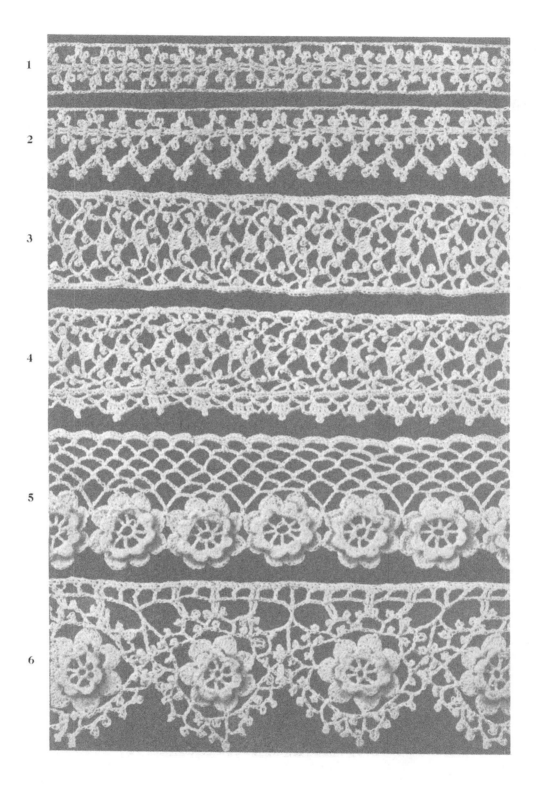

1

2

3

4

5

6

Irish Beauties

Make your home—your gowns—your children's clothing sparkle with these lovely frosted edgings

**Materials Suggested — AMERICAN THREAD COMPANY
"STAR" TATTING COTTON or "STAR" or "GEM"
MERCERIZED CROCHET COTTON
Sizes 50 or 70**

No. 1

Insertion

Ch 7, sl st in 6th st from hook for picot, * ch 6, sl st in 5th st from hook for picot, repeat from * ch 1, 2 d c in 1st st of ch 7, ** turn work, * ch 6, sl st in 5th st for picot, repeat from * twice, ch 1, 1 d c in each d c, repeat from ** for length desired. **2nd Row**. Join thread in center picot, ch 5, s c in center picot of next group. Repeat ch on other side of insertion.

No. 2

Edging. Repeat 1st row of insertion and work a 5 ch loop on one side same as on insertion. On other side, join thread in center picot, ** ch 5, d c in first st of ch, * ch 4, sl st in 4th st from hook for picot, repeat from * twice sl st in side of 1st picot, ch 5, d c in 1st st of ch, sl st in center picot of next group and repeat from ** across row.

No. 3

Ch 22, s c in 9th st from hook, * ch 6, skip 2 chs, s c in next ch, repeat from * twice, ch 3, skip 2 chs, d c in next ch, turn.

2nd Row. Ch 8, sl st in 4th st from hook for picot, ch 6, sl st in 4th st from hook for picot, ch 2, s c in next 6 ch loop, ch 4, 5 d c in next loop, ch 4, s c in next loop, * ch 6, sl st in 4th st from hook for picot, repeat from * ch 3, s c in end loop, turn.

3rd Row. Ch 7, s c between next 2 picots, * ch 6, sl st in 4th st from hook for picot, repeat from * ch 2, skip 2 d c, s c in next d c, double picot loop, ch 2, s c between next 2 picots, ch 3, skip 1 ch after picot, d c in next ch, ch 7, turn.

4th Row. S c in 1st 3 ch loop, * ch 6, s c between next 2 picots, repeat from * ch 6, s c in next loop, ch 3, d c in same loop, turn and repeat from 2nd row for length desired.

Work a row of s c on each side of insertion working about 4 s c in each loop.

No. 4

Repeat directions for insertion and across one side work the following scallop.

* Ch 5, skip 3 s c, sl st in next st, repeat from * across row, turn.

Next Row. Ch 3, 2 d c, picot, 2 d c in same loop, * ch 3, s c in next loop, ch 3, 3 d c, picot, 2 d c in next loop, repeat from * across row.

No. 5

Rose. Ch 7, join to form a ring, ch 6, d c in ring, * ch 3, d c in ring, repeat from * 5 times, ch 3, join in 3rd st of ch 6.

2nd Row. Ch 1 and work 1 s c, 3 d c, 1 s c in each mesh. **3rd Row**. S1 st into back of d c of previous row, * ch 6.

sl st over next d c of previous row, repeat from * 7 times.

4th Row. Ch 1, l s c, 7 d c, 1 s c in each loop.

Work a 2nd rose joining in the last row as follows: 1 s c, 4 d c, join to center st of petal of 1st rose with a si st, 3 d c, 1 s c in same loop, 1 s c, 4 d c in next loop, join to center st of next petal of 1st rose, 3 d c, 1 s c in same loop and finish rose same as 1st rose.

Join all roses in same manner leaving 2 free petals on each side.

Heading. Join thread in center of 1st free petal, * ch 7, s c in center of next petal, ch 7, s c in joining of petals, ch 7, s c in center of 1st petal in next flower and repeat from * across row, ch 9, turn. **2nd Row**. S c in loop * ch 7, s c in next loop, repeat from * across row, ch 9 and work 4 more rows of loops. **6th Row. 7** s c in each loop.

No. 6

Ch 6, join to form a ring, ch 6, d c into ring, * ch 3, d c into ring, repeat from * 4 times, ch 3, join in 3rd st of ch.

2nd Row. Ch 1, 1 s c, 3 d c, 1 s c over each loop. 3rd Row. Sl st in d c of 1st row in back of petal, * ch 8, sl st in next d c in back of petal, repeat from * all around.

4th Row. Ch 1, 1 s c, 7 d c, 1 s c in each loop. 5th Row. Sl st to center of petal, * ch 7, sl st in 5th st for picot, repeat from *, ch 2, s c in center of next petal, repeat all around.

6th Row. Sl st to center of double picot loop, * ch 7, sl st in 5th st for picot, repeat from * ch 2, d c in s c, double picot loop, s c in center of next double picot loop and repeat from 1set * all around, break thread. Work a second Motif joining it to 1st Motif in the last row as follows—work 1 double picot loop, d c in s c, ch 7, sl st in 5th st for picot, ch 1, sl st into corresponding loop of 1st Motif, ch 6, sl st in 5th st for picot, ch 2, s c between next 2 picots of Motifs being made, ch 7, sl st in 5th st for picot, ch 1, sl st in corresponding loop of 1st Motif, ch 6, sl st in 5th st for picot, cli 2 and complete 2nd Motif.

Work as many Motifs as desired joining them in same manner leaving 5 double picot loops free between joinings.

Heading. Join thread between picots of center double picot loop, ch 3, d c in same space, * ch 7, 2 tr c in center of next double picot loop, ch 7, thread over 3 times, insert in center of next loop and work off 2 loops twice, thread over 3 times, insert in joining of Motifs and work off 2 loops 3 times, thread over twice, insert in center of 1st loop of next Motif and work off all loops 2 at a time, ch 7, 2 tr c in next loop, ch 7, 2 d c in next loop and repeat from *.

2nd Row. Ch 3, d c in d c, ch 3, d c in center st of loop, ch 3, 1 d c in each tr c, ch 3, d c in center st of loop, ch 3, tr c in d tr c cluster, ch 3, d c in center st of next loop, ch 3, 1 d c in each tr c, ch 3, d c in center st of next loop, ch 3 and continue all around.

3rd Row. 1 s c in each d c and tr c and 2 s c in each mesh.

Dublin Beauty Bedspread

Materials Required—
AMERICAN THREAD COMPANY
"PURITAN" MERCERIZED CROCHET
AND KNITTING COTTON

52 300-yd. Balls White, Ecru, Cream or Beige.

Motif measures about 5½ inches. 262 Motifs are required for Spread measuring about 72 x 110 inches without fringe.

Steel Crochet Hook No. 7.

MOTIF. Ch 6, join to form a ring, ch 3, 3 d c in ring. slip loop off hook, insert in 3rd st of ch and pull through, * ch 4, 4 d c in ring, sl loop off hook, insert in first d c and pull through, (popcorn st) repeat from * twice, ch 4, join in 1st popcorn st.

2nd Row—Sl st to next loop and over each loop work 1 s c, 4 d c, 1 s c.

3rd Row—Ch 4 and working in back of petal into the first row, s c in lower center edge of petal, ch 4, s c between petals, repeat from beginning all around. (8 loops)

4th Row—Over each loop work 1 s c, 5 d c, 1 s c. 5th Row—Ch 1 and working in back of petal, s c in lower center edge of petal, * ch 5, s c in center of next petal, repeat from * all around. (8 loops)

6th Row—Over each loop work 1 s c, 7 d c, 1 s c.

7th Row—S c in s c of 5th row, * ch 9, s c in 2nd st from hook, 1 s d c in each of the next 2 sts, (s d c: thread over needle, insert in st and work off all loops at one time) 1 d c in each of the next 3 sts, 1 tr c in each of the next 2 sts, s c in next s c in 5th row between petals and repeat from * all around. (8 leaves)

8th Row—Work 7 s c on side of next leaf, 3 s c in point of leaf, 7 s c on other side of leaf and repeat on all leaves.

9th Row—S1 st to point of next leaf, * ch 7, thread over twice, insert in 5th s c on side of same leaf, work off 2 loops twice, thread over twice, insert in corresponding s c on next leaf and work off all loops 2 at a time, ch 7, s c in point of next leaf and repeat from * all around.

10th Row—S1 st to loop, ch 3, work 7 d c in 1st loop and 8 d c in each remaining loop, join.

11th Row—Ch 9, s c between next 2 groups of d c, repeat from beginning all around.

12th Row—S1 st into loop, ch 3, (ch 3 at the beginning of a row counts as 1 d c) thread over, insert in loop and work off 2 loops, thread over, insert in loop and work off 2 loops 3 times, (a cluster st) ch 3, * 3 d c cluster st in same loop, (work off last 3 loops at one time) repeat from * 3 times, ** ch 5, 3 s c in next loop, ch 7, 3 s c in next loop, ch 7, 3 s c in next loop, ch 5, 5 cluster sts with ch 3 between each cluster st in next loop, repeat from ** all around, join in 1st cluster st.

13th Row—Sl st between 1st 2 cluster sts, * ch 5, cluster st in next loop, ch 3, cluster st in next loop, ch 5, s c in next loop, ch 5, s c in next loop, ch 7, 3 s c in next loop, ch 7, 3 s c in next loop, ch 7, s c in next loop, ch 5, s c in next loop, repeat from * all around.

14th Row—Sl st to center of loop, ch 5, cluster st in next loop, ch 9, sl st in top of cluster st for picot, ch 5, s c in next loop, ch 6, s c in next loop, * ch 6, 3 s c in next loop, repeat from * twice, ch 6, s c in next loop, ch 6, s c in next loop, repeat from beginning all around. Motifs are joined in the last row as follows: Work one side of last row to corner, ch 5, cluster st in corner loop, ch 4, sl st in picot of 1st motif, ch 4, complete picot, ch 5, s c in next loop, ch 4, sl st in center st of corresponding loop of 1st motif, ch 4, s c in next loop, * ch 4, sl st in center st of next loop of 1st motif, ch 4, 3 s c in next loop, repeat from * twice, * ch 4, sl st in next loop of 1st motif, ch 4, s c in next loop of 2nd motif, repeat from * once, ch 5, work a cluster st in next loop, join picots and complete motif. Join all motifs in same manner, having 3 rows of 17 motifs, 8 rows of 20 motifs (adding all motifs on one side for shaping at lower edge) and 3 rows of 17 motifs.

Edge. Attach thread on side and ** work 5 d c in each of the first 3 loops, * 1 d c in each of the next 3 s c, 5 d c in next loop, repeat from * twice, 5 d c in each of the next 2 loops, 4 d c in each of the next 2 loops, repeat from ** all around.

2nd Row—Ch 5, skip 2 d c, d c in next d c, * ch 2, skip 2 d c, d c in next d c, repeat from * across side, break thread.

Work 2 ch meshes across lower edge and work other side to correspond. Do not work meshes on sides of corner shaping.

Fringe. Cut 12 strands 15 inches long, double these and knot into mesh. Repeat in every other mesh across each side and lower edge.

Irish Springtime

Materials Required—AMERICAN THREAD COMPANY "STAR" MERCERIZED CROCHET COTTON

2—175 Yd. Balls, Size 50, White.

Steel Crochet Hook No. 13.

Doily measures 10 inches.

Ch 6, join to form a ring, ch 6, d c in ring, * ch 3, d c in ring, repeat from * 3 times, ch 3, join in 3rd st of ch.

2nd Row. Ch 1, * 2 d c, 5 tr c, 2 d c in next mesh, s c in next d c, repeat from * all around.

3rd Row. * Ch 6, s c in next s c in back of petal, repeat from * all around.

4th Row. In each loop work 2 d c, 8 tr c, 2 d c, s c in s c between petals.

5th Row. Sl st to 2nd tr c, * ch 7, sl st in 5th st from hook for picot, ch 7, sl st in 5th st from hook for picot, ch 2, skip 4 tr c, s c in next tr c, ch 7, sl st in 5th st from hook for picot, ch 7, sl st in 5th st from hook for picot, ch 2, s c in 2nd tr c of next scallop, repeat from * all around.

6th Row. Ch 8, * s c between next 2 picots, ch 5, d c in next s c, ch 5, repeat from * all around ending row with s c between next 2 picots, ch 5, join in 3rd st of ch.

7th Row. Sl st into loop, ch 3, 3 d c in same space, ch 1, 4 d c in next loop, ch 3, s c in next loop, ch 5, s c in next loop, ch 3, * 4 d c in next loop, ch 1, 4 d c in next loop, ch 3, s c in next loop, ch 5, s c in next loop, ch 3, repeat from * all around, join.

8th Row. Ch 5, s c in ch 1 between d c groups, ch 5, skip 3 d c, s c in next d c, double picot loop, skip the 3 ch loop, s c in next loop, double picot loop, skip the 3 ch loop, s c in 1st d c of next d c group, repeat from beginning all around.

9th Row. Sl st to loop, ch 3, 3 d c in same space, * ch 1, 4 d c in next loop, ch 5, s c between next 2 picots, ch 5, d c in s c at base of loop, ch 5, s c between next 2 picots, ch 5, 4 d c in next loop, repeat from * all around.

10th Row. Ch 5, s c in ch 1 between d c group, ch 5, skip 3 d c, s c in next d c, double picot loop, skip 1 loop, s c in next loop, double picot loop, s c in next loop, double picot loop, skip 1 loop, s c in next d c, repeat from beginning all around.

11th Row. Sl st to loop, ch 3, 3 d c in same loop, ** ch 1, 4 d c in next loop, * ch 5, s c between next 2 picots, ch 5, d c in s c at base of loop, repeat from *, ch 5, s c between next 2 picots, ch 5, 4 d c in next loop, repeat from ** all around, join.

12th Row. Same as 10th row having 5 double picot loops between sections.

13th Row. Sl st to loop, ch 3, 3 d c in same space, ch 1, 4 d c in next loop, * ch 5, s c between next 2 picots of next loop, repeat from * 4 times, ch 5, 4 d c in next loop, repeat all around.

14th Row. Same as 12th row.

15th Row. Same as 13th row having 6 chs in each loop.

16th Row. Same as 12th row.

17th Row. Same as 13th row having 7 chs in each loop.

18th Row. Same as 12th row.

19th Row. Sl st to loop, ch 3, 3 d c in same loop, ch 1, 4 d c in next loop, ch 6, * s c between next 2 picots, ch 6, d c in s c at base of loop, ch 6, repeat from *, ch 7, skip the 2 picots, d c in s c at base of loop, ch 6, s c between next 2 picots, ch 6, d c in s c at base of loop, ch 6, s c between next 2 picots, ch 6, 4 d c over next loop, repeat all around.

20th Row. Double picot loop, s c in ch 1 between d c groups, double picot loop, skip 3 d c, s c in next d c, double picot loop, skip I loop, s c in next loop, * double picot loop, s c in next loop, repeat from *, 9 d c in next loop, s c in next loop, double picot loop, s c in next loop, double picot loop, s c in next loop, double picot loop, skip 1 loop, s c in 1st d c of next d c group, repeat from beginning all around.

21st Row. Sl st between picots, * ch 7, s c between picots of next loop, repeat from * 3 times, ** ch 7, s c in center st of d c group, * ch 7, s c between picots of next loop, repeat from * 7 times, repeat from ** all around.

22nd Row. Sl st to center of loop, * double picot loop, s c in next loop, repeat from * twice. double picot loop, ** s c in next loop, 7 d c in same loop, s c in same loop, ch 1, s c, 7 d c, s c in next loop, * double picot loop, s c in next loop, repeat from * 6 times, double picot loop, repeat from ** all around ending row with the 4 double picot loops.

23rd Row. Sl st between picots, * ch 7, s c between picots of next loop, repeat from * twice, ch 7, s c in center d c of petal, ch 7, s c in center d c of next scallop, * ch 7, s c between picots of next loop, repeat from * 7 times, ch 7, s c in center st of next petal, ch 7, s c in center st of next petal, repeat all around.

24th Row. Sl st to loop, * double picot loop, s c in next loop, repeat from * twice, ** double picot loop, s c in next loop, 9 d c in same loop, s c in same loop, * double picot loop, s c in next loop, repeat from * 8 times, then repeat from ** all around, ending row with 6 double picot loops.

25th Row. Sl st between picots, * ch 7, s c between picots of next loop, repeat from * twice, ** ch 7, s c in center st of petal, * ch 7, s c between picots of next loop, repeat from * 9 times, repeat from ** all around.

26th Row. Work double picot loops, working l s c, 9 d c, 1 s c in each of the 2 loops over petal of previous row.

27th Row. Sl st between picots, ch 7, s c between picots of next loop, ch 7, s c between picots of next loop, ** ch 7, s c in center st of petal, ch 7, sc in center st of next petal, * ch 7, s c between picots of next loop, repeat from * 9 times, repeat from ** all around and work 1 row of double picot loops even, break thread.

Flowers. Ch 6, join to form a ring, ch 6, d c in ring, * ch 3, d c in ring, repeat from * 3 times, ch 3, join in 3rd st of ch.

Next Row. Ch 1, 1 s d c, 1 d c, 3 tr c, 1 d c, l s d c in next mesh, s c in d c, 1 s d c, 1 d c, 2 tr c in next mesh, ch 2, join between picots of any loop, ch 2, sl st in tr c just made, l tr c, 1 d c, l s d c in same space, s c in d c, 1 s d c, 1 d c, 2 tr c in next mesh, ch 2, join between picots of next loop, ch 2, sl st in top of tr c just made, 1 tr c, 1 d c, 1 s d c in same space, s c in d c, * 1 s d c, 1 d c, 3 tr c, 1 d c, 1 s d c in next mesh, s c in d c, repeat from * all around, break thread.

Work another flower in same manner joining it between picots to the next 2 loops of doily and joining side petals together with a sl st. Work 34 more flowers always joining 2 petals to next 2 loops of doily and joining side petals to side petal of previous flower leaving 2 petals free at top and joining last flower to 1st flower at side petal.

Irish Crochet Edgings

J. & P. Coats Big Ball Best Six Cord Mercerized Crochet, Art. A.104, or Clark's Big Ball Mercerized Crochet, Art. B.34 ... use Size 50 with Milwards Steel Crochet Hook No. 12, or use Size 70 with Milwards Steel Crochet Hook No. 14, or use Size 100 with Milwards Steel Crochet Hook No. 16.

Irish Crochet Edgings

Illustrated on page 40

S-832 FIRST MOTIF ... Starting at center, ch 8. Join with sl st to form ring. **1st rnd:** Make 12 sc in ring. Join. **2nd rnd:** Sc in same place as sl st, * ch 5, skip 1 sc, sc in next sc. Repeat from * around, ending with ch 5. Join to first sc. **3rd rnd:** In each loop around make sc, half dc, 5 dc, half dc and sc. Join. **4th rnd:** * (Ch 5, sc in 3rd ch from hook—picot made) twice; ch 2, sc in the sc on 2nd rnd between next 2 petals. Repeat from * around. Break off.

SECOND MOTIF ... Work as for First Motif until 4 rnds have been completed but do not break off thread.

To join, work in rows as follows: **1st row:** Sl st to center of next picot loop, sc in same place, (ch 2, picot) twice and ch 2; sc in center of next picot loop. Turn. **2nd row:** (Ch 2, picot) twice and ch 2; sc in center of next picot loop, (ch 2, picot) twice and ch 2; sc in sc at base of picot loop on previous row. Turn. **3rd row:** Sl st to center of next picot loop, sc in same place, (ch 2, picot) twice and ch 2; sc in next picot loop. Turn. **4th row:** Ch 2, picot, ch 1, sl st in any free loop on First Motif, ch 4, sc in 3rd ch from hook, ch 2, sc in next picot loop, ch 2, join next picot loop on First Motif as before, ch 4, make a ch-3 picot and ch 2, sc in sc at base of previous row. Break off.

Make necessary number of motifs for length desired, joining as Second Motif was joined to First Motif, leaving one free picot loop on each side of joining.

HEADING . . . Attach thread to center picot loop of Motif and work across long side as follows: Sc in same place, * (ch 5, dc in next picot loop) 4 times; ch 5, sc in next picot loop. Repeat from * across., ending to correspond with beginning. Break off.

SCALLOPED EDGE . . . Skip a loop at outside edge of Motif, attach thread to center of next loop, ch 2, picot, ch 3, * in the center of next free loop make (tr, ch 3, sc in tip of tr) 7 times; ch 5, sc in next free picot loop, (ch 2, picot) twice; ch 2, sc in next loop, ch 5. Repeat from " across, ending with ch 3, picot and ch 2; sc in next picot loop. Break off.

S-833 FIRST SHAMROCK . . . Starting at center, ch 29. **1st rnd:** Sl st in 14th ch from hook, (ch 13, sl st in same ch) twice. **2nd rnd:** Working over 1 strand of "Speed-Cro-Sheen," make 25 sc in each loop, then, still working over "Speed-Cro-Sheen," make 15 sc over remainder of chain for stem, having last sc in end ch. Cut off "Speed-Cro-Sheen." **3rd rnd:** Sc in same place as last sc, (ch 7, sc in 4th ch from hook—picot made—ch 3, skip 9 sc on next petal, sc in next sc, ch 3, picot, ch 3, skip 5 sc, sc in next sc, ch 3, picot, ch 3, tr between this petal and next petal) twice; ch 3, picot, ch 3, skip 9 sc on next peta', sc in next sc, ch 3, picot, ch 3, skip 5 sc, sc in next sc, ch 3, picot, ch 3, sc in center sc on stem, ch 3, picot, ch 3, sl st in first sc. Break off.

SECOND SHAMROCK ... Work as for First Shamrock until picot loops have been worked around 2nd petal, ending with tr, ch 3, picot, ch 3, skip 9 sc on next petal, sc in next sc, ch 5, sl st in corresponding picot loop of First Shamrock, ch 2, sc in 4tr3 ch of ch-5, ch 3, skip 5 sc on Second Shamrock, sc in next sc. Complete rnd as before (no more joinings).

Make necessary number of Shamrocks until piece measures length desired.

HEADING ... 1st row: With wrong side facing, attach thread to 2nd picot preceding joining on First Shamrock, sc in same place, * ch 11, holding back on hook the last loop of each tr, make tr in next 2 picots, thread over and draw through all loops on hook (joint tr made), ch 11, sc in next picot. Repeat from * across, ending with sc. Ch 4, turn. **2nd row:** * (Skip 1 ch, dc in next ch, ch 1) 5 times; skip 1 ch, dc in next st, ch 1. Repeat from ” across. Break off.

S-834 FIRST LEAF ... Starting at center, ch 16. **1st rnd: Sc** in 2nd ch from hook and in each ch across, 3 sc in last ch; working along opposite side of starting chain, make sc in each ch across, 2 sc in same ch as first sc was made.

Hereafter pick up back loops only. Work is now done in rows. **1st row:** Sc in each sc across to within 1 sc of next 3-sc group. Ch 1, turn. **2nd row:** Sc in each sc across, making 3 sc in center sc of 3-sc group, sc in each remaining sc to within 1 sc of next 3-sc group. Ch 1, turn. **3rd to 6th rows incl:** Sc in each sc across to within last 3 sc, making 3 sc in center sc of 3-sc group. Ch 1, turn. **7th row:** Sc in each sc across to center sc of 3-sc group, sl st in center sc. Break off.

SECOND LEAF ... Work as for First Leaf until 6 rows have been completed. Ch 1, turn. **7th row:** Sl st in corresponding sc on First Leaf, sc in each sc across to center sc of 3-sc group, sl st in center sc. Break off.

Make necessary number of leaves for length desired.

HEADING ... **1st row:** Attach thread to center sc of First Leaf, sc in same place, * ch 7, holding back on hook the last loop of each tr, make a tr in center sc on side of this leaf and in corresponding sc on next leaf, thread over and draw through all loops on hook (joint tr made), ch 7, sc in center sc of same leaf. Repeat from * across. Ch

4, turn. **2nd row:** * Skip 1 st, dc in next st, ch 1. Repeat from * across. Break off.

S-835 FIRST MOTIF ... Starting at center, ch 6. Join with sl st to form ring. **1st rnd:** (Sc in ring, ch 12) 4 times. Join to first sc. **2nd rnd:** Working over a strand of "Speed-Cro-Sheen" make 20 sc in first loop, * sl st in ring, 20 sc in next loop. Repeat from * around. Join to first sc. Break off. **3rd rnd:** Attach thread to 8th sc on any petal, sc in same place, * ch 6, sc in 3rd ch from hook (picot made), ch 3, skip 4 sc, sc in next sc, ch 3, picot, ch 3, skip 7 sc on next loop, sc in next sc. Repeat from * around. Join to first sc. **4th rnd:** Sl st in next ch and in same loop, ch 8, dc in same loop on other side of picot, * ch 3, in next loop make sc, ch 5 and sc; ch 3, in next loop make dc, ch 5 and dc. Repeat from * around. Join to 3rd ch of ch-8. Break off.

SECOND MOTIF . . . Work as for First Motif until 3 rnds have been completed. **4th rnd:** Sl st in next ch and in same loop, ch 8, dc in same loop, ch 3, in next loop make sc, ch 5 and sc; ch 3, dc in next loop, ch 2, sl st in corresponding loop on First Motif, ch 2, dc in same loop on Second Motif. Complete rnd (no more joinings).

Make necessary number of motifs for length desired.

HEADING ... 1st row: Attach thread to 3rd ch-5 loop preceding joining on First Motif, sc in same place, * ch 5, in next ch-5 loop make sc, ch 5 and sc; ch 5, sc in next ch-5 loop, ch 12, sc in corresponding loop on next motif, turn; make 15 sc in last ch-12 loop made, turn; sc in first sc, (ch 3, skip 1 sc, sc in next sc) 7 times; sl st in same ch-5 loop. Repeat from * across, ending with sc in ch-5 loop. Ch 13, turn. **2nd row:** Skip first loop, sc in next loop, ch 10, skip 2 ch-3 loops, (sc in next loop, ch 3) twice; sc in next loop, ch 10, skip next ch-5 loop, sc in next loop. Repeat from * across, ending with ch 10, dc in last sc. Break off.

SCALLOPED EDGE ... 1st row: Skip 3 loops following Heading on First Motif, attach thread to next loop, sc in same place, * ch 3, picot, ch 3, skip next loop,in next loop make sc, ch 3, picot, ch 3 and sc, ch 3, picot, ch 3, skip next loop, sc in next loop, ch 3, holding back on hook the last loop of each dc make dc in next loop and in corresponding loop on next motif, thread over and draw through all loops on hook (joint dc made), ch 3, sc in next loop. Repeat from * across. Break off.

S-836 Starting at long side, make a chain slightly longer than length desired.

FIRST POINT . . . 1st row: Dc in 8th ch from hook, (ch 2, skip 2 ch, dc in next ch) twice. Ch 5, turn. **2nd row:** Skip first dc, sc in next dc, ch 5, sc in next dc, ch 5, skip 2 ch, sc in next ch. Turn. **3rd row:** 7 sc in next 2 loops, 4 sc in next loop. Ch 5, turn. **4th row:** Sc in center sc of next loop, ch 5, sc in center sc of next loop. Turn. **5th row:** 7 sc in first loop, 4 sc in next loop. Ch 5, turn. **6th row:** Sc in center sc of next loop. Turn. **7th row:** In ch-5 loop make 2 sc, (ch 3, sc) twice, ch 3 and 2 sc; then make 3 sc in each incompleted loop along side of point, sl st in last dc made, (ch 2, skip 2 ch, dc in next ch) 4 times. Ch 5, turn. Repeat 2nd to 7th rows incl until piece measures length desired, ending with sl st in last dc made. Break off.

S-837 Starting at narrow end, ch 11. **1st row:** In 11th ch from hook make dc, ch 3 and de. Ch 7, turn. **2nd row:** Dc in ch-3 sp, ch 3, sc in 3rd ch from hook (picot made), in same sp make (dc, picot) 3 times and dc.Ch 10, turn. **3rd row:** Skip 2 dc, in next dc make dc, ch 3 and dc. Ch 7, turn. Repeat 2nd and 3rd rows alternately until piece measures length desired, ending with 2nd row. Break off.

HEADING . . . Attach thread to first ch-10 loop and, working across long side, make sc in same loop, * ch 6, sc in next loop. Repeat from * across. Break off.

SCALLOPED EDGE . . . Attach thread to first ch-7 loop on opposite side, ch 6, sc in 3rd ch from hook, in same loop make (dc, picot) 3 times and dc; * in next loop make (dc, picot) 4 times and dc. Repeat from * across. Break off.

S-838 FIRST MOTIF ... Starting at center, ch 8. Join with sl st to form ring. **1st rnd:** Working over 1 strand of "Speed-Cro-Sheen," make 18 sc in ring. Sl st in first sc. Drop "Speed-Cro-Sheen." **2nd rnd:** Sc in same place as sl st, * ch 5, skip 2 sc, sc in next sc. Repeat from * around, ending with sl st in first sc (6 loops). **3rd rnd:** Sc in next loop, * ch 5, in same loop make (tr, ch 1) 3 times and tr; ch 5, sc in same loop, sc in next loop. Repeat from * around (6 petals). **4th rnd:** Working over "Speed-Cro-Sheen," * make 5 sc in ch-5 on side of petal, 2 sc in each of next 3 sps, 5 sc in next ch-5. Repeat from * around. Join and break off.

SECOND MOTIF . . . Work as for First Motif until 3rd rnd has been completed. **4th rnd:** Working over "Speed-Cro-Sheen," make 5 sc in ch-5 on side of petal, 2 sc in next sp, sc in next sp, sl st in center sc of any petal of First Motif, sc in same sp on Second Motif, 2 sc in next sp, 5 sc in ch-5 on other side of petal. Complete rnd as for First Motif (no more joinings) and break off.

Make necessary number of motifs, joining as for Second Motif, leaving 2 petals free between joinings.

HEADING . . . 1st row: Attach thread to center of second free petal preceding joining on First Motif, sc in same place, * ch 10, sc in center of next petal, ch 4, skip 3 sc, holding back on hook the last loop of each tr make tr in next sc and in corresponding sc of first petal of next motif, thread over and draw through all loops on hook, ch 4, sc in center sc of same petal. Repeat from * across. Ch 4, turn. **2nd row:** Skip 1 ch, dc in next ch, * ch l, skip 1 st, dc in next st.

Repeat from * across. Ch 4, turn. **3rd row:** Skip first dc, * dc in next dc, ch 1. Repeat from * across, ending with ch 1, skip 1 ch of turning chain, dc in next ch. Break off.

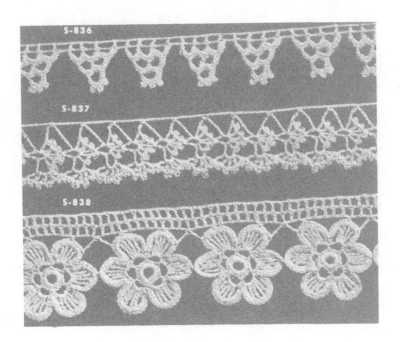

A Block a Day

MATERIALS—Lily Homestead Crochet and Knitting Cotton, Art. 131 in skeins or Art. 205 in balls, and Lily Skytone Mercerized Crochet Cotton, Art. 123, in a color:—SINGLE SIZE—9—sks. Ecru or 12-sks. White; or 8-balls Ecru or 9-balls White or Cream; and 21-balls Skytone in desired color. DOUBLE SIZE—12—sks. Ecru or 15-sks. White; or 10-balls Ecru or 12-balls White or Cream; and 26-balls Skytone in desired color. GAUGE—Each Block measures about 6½" square (9" diagonally across corners). For single size spread about 63" x 108", make 150 Blocks; for double size spread about 81" x 108", make 196 Blocks. Crochet hook size 10. BLOCK—In Homestead Cotton, (ch 6, sl st in one lp of 4th st from hook for a p) 6 times, remove hook from lp, insert it back in starting st, catch lp and pull thru to form a circle with all ps on inside of ring. Ch 3 and working over starting thread end, make 1 dc at base of last p, ch 4, sl st in dc for a p, 1 dc in same p, * (2 dc, a p and 1 dc) in next sp on ring between ps, (2 dc, a p and 1 dc) at base of next p. Repeat from * around. Sl st in top of 1st 3-ch. ROW 2—Ch 8, dc between next 2 ps, (ch 5, dc between next 2 ps) 10 times, ch 5, sl st in 3d st of 1st 8-ch. ROW 3—(7 sc in next 1p) 12 times, sl st in 1st sc, cut 6" long, thread to a needle and fasten off on back. ROW 4—Sc in colored Skytone in same sc with sl st, * ch 1, dc in next sc, tr in next, 3 tr in next, 1 tr in next, dc in next, ch 1, sc in next, sc in 1st sc on next lp. Repeat from * around, sl st in 1st sc and fasten off. ROW 5 —In Homestead Cotton, sl st in one lp of center tr of next (1st) petal, ch 9, sc thru 2 left-hand lps of 4th st from hook for a p, ch 1, tr in same tr, (ch 4, p, ch 1, tr in same st) 3 times, * ch 5, p, ch 2, sc in next petal, ch 5, p, ch 9, p, ch 2, sc in next petal, ch 5, p, ch 2, tr in one lp of center tr of next petal, (ch 4, p, ch 1, tr in same st) 5 times. Repeat from * around. End with 1 tr to complete 1st shell, ch 4, p, ch 1, sl st in 5th st of 1st p-lp. ROW 6—Ch 10, p, ch 2, tr in next tr, (ch 5, p, ch 2, tr in next tr) twice, * ch 5, p, ch 2, dc in next tr, ch 5, p, ch 9, p, ch 2, sc in next p-1p, ch 5, p, ch 9, p, ch 2, dc in next tr, (ch 5, p, ch 2, tr in next tr) 4 times. Repeat from * around. Join final p-lp to 5th st of 1st p-1p. ROW 7—* Ch 6, p, ch 9, p, ch 3, tr in next tr, ch 14, (tr in side-top of last tr and tr in next tr) holding back the last lp of each tr on hook, thread over and pull thru all 3 lps at once for a Cluster, ch 6, p, ch 9, p, ch 3, sc in next tr, (ch 6, p, ch 9, p, ch 3, sc in next p-1p) twice, ch 6, p, ch 9, p, ch 3, sc in next tr. Repeat from * around. Fasten off. EDGE—Join colored Skytone to 5th st of one corner 14-ch lp, ch 3, (3 dc, ch 5, 4 dc) in same st, * ch 12, sl st in starting st of 12-ch, (4 dc, ch 5, 4 dc) in next 5th st of corner lp, (4 dc in one lp of 3d st between ps of next lp, ch 5, 4 dc in one lp of next st) 5 times, (4 dc, ch 5, 4 dc) in one lp of 5th st of corner lp. Repeat from * around. Sl st in 1st 3-ch and fasten off.

Make and join Blocks by the corner lps and by the 7 shells on each side of Edge Row:—To join, in place of a corner 12-ch lp, make 6-ch, sl st in one lp of center st of a corner lp on another Block, ch 5, sk last 5 sts of 6-ch, sl st back in next st. Repeat at each corner. To join shells, in place of center 5-ch lp, make 2-ch, sl st in corresponding shell on another Block, ch 2 back and complete shell with 4 dc. Repeat with each shell.

For a single size spread, join 7 rows of Blocks (12 Blocks in each row) by the corners. Then fill in openings between rows with 6 rows of Blocks (11 Blocks in each row).

For a double size spread, join 9 rows of Blocks (12 Blocks in each row) by corners. Fill in openings between rows with 8 rows of Blocks (11 Blocks in each row).

Block to measurements given.

TASSEL—Wind 2 strands colored Skytone 36 times around a 6" card. Cut at one edge. Tie a 15" strand tightly around center, thread one end to a needle, fold tassel in center, take needle down thru tassel ⅝", wrap tightly 3 times around tassel and fasten securely. Insert crochet hook under tie strand at top of tassel, catch other end of tie strand, pull thru, ch 5 and pull thru, thread to a needle and fasten to edge of spread. Fasten a tassel to each point and between points on both sides of spread and across bottom edge. Trim tassels to an even length.

Simplified Irish Crochet

No. 23—IRISH CROCHET BANDED DINNER TABLE DOILY

SIZE—12½ x 17 inches.

MATERIALS—Lily SIX CORD Mercerized Crochet Cotton, size 30.

BAND—Ch 79, dc in 7th st from hook, (ch 6, sc in 5th st from hook for a p, ch 2, dc in next 8th st of long ch, ch 3, dc in same st) 9 times.
ROW2—Ch 1, turn, sl st in 2d st of last 3-ch, ch 6, dc in same st, (ch 6, p, ch 2, sk next p-loop, dc in 2d st of 3-ch between next 2 dc, ch 3, dc in same st) 8 times, ch 6, p, ch 2, dc in 2d st of end 6-ch, ch 3, dc in same st. Repeat this row until Band measures (stretched) about 15¾ inches. Ch l, turn, sl st in 2d st of last 3-ch, ch 6, dc in same st, (ch 4, sk next p, dc in 2d st of 3-ch between next 2 dc, ch 3, dc in same st) repeated to end of row. Now work down long side of Band with 4 sc in each space, 3 sc in corner st, 7 sc in each space across

end, 3 sc in corner st, 4 sc in each space on long side, 7 sc in corner space, 4 sc in each 4-ch and 3 sc in each 3-ch across end. Fasten off. Stretch and pin Band right-side-down on an ironing board and steam with a wet cloth and hot iron, then press thru a dry cloth until perfectly dry.

FLOWER—Wind thread 16 times around the ends of 2 crochet hooks held together. Slip off and cover ring with 20 sc. Sl st in 1st sc. **ROW 2**—(Ch 3, sc in next sc) 20 times. Sl st to center of 1st loop. **ROW 3**—(Ch 3, sc in next loop) 20 times. Sl st to center of 1st loop. **ROW 4**—Ch 3 for a dc, 5 dc in same loop, remove hook, insert in top of 3-ch, catch loop and pull thru (Popcorn Stitch). (Ch 3, a 6-dc-Popcorn in next loop) 19 times. Ch 3, sl st in 1st Popcorn. **ROW 5**— 3 sc over each 3-ch space. Sl st in 1st sc and fasten off. **ROW 6**— Repeat Row I. Fasten off. Make 12 of these rings. Tack one to every 5th sc on Row 5. Tack rings to each other. Make 3 Flowers.

RING GROUPS—Repeat Row 1 of Flower. Make 4 of these rings and tack together. Make 2 of these Groups.

LEAF SPRAY—Ch 4, making 1st st extra long by pushing it up over flat place on hook, (3 tr, 13 dtr and 3 tr) in this long st, ch 3, sc in same place. Ch 3. and working in back loops, make 1 sc in 1st tr, 2 sc in next 18 sts, ch 3, sc in sc at base of Leaf. Ch 2 and working in back loops, make sc in next sc, * ch 2, 1 dc in next, 3 dc in next, 1 dc in next. ch 2, sc in next. Repeat from * 8 times. Ch 2, sl st at base of Leaf. (Ch 5, 3 dc in 5th st from hook, holding last loop of each dc on hook, thread over and pull thru all 4 loops on hook at once) 6 times. Fasten off. Make 2 more Leaves with only 2 Clusters on each for stems. Attach these 2 Leaves to stem of 1st Leaf—1 on each side— between 4th and 5th Clusters from Leaf. Make a 2d Leaf Spray. Tack motifs on Band, following illustration. Cut a piece of linen to fit Band, hem and whip to lace.

EDGE—Join to upper right corner of **Band**, to the 1st of 7 sc in corner space, ch 4, tr in corner st, (ch 2. tr in same st) 5 times, ch 4, sk 3 sc, sc in next 5 sc, * ch 4, tr in next 6th sc, (ch 2, tr in same st) 3 times, ch 4, sk 5 sc, sc in next 5 sc. Repeat from * around Doily, working into edge of linen, and spacing shells so that each corner is the same as 1st one. **ROW 2**—5 sc over 1st 4-ch, (2 sc, ch 5, sl st in last sc for a p, and I sc) in each of next five 2-ch spaces, 5 sc in next 4-ch, * sk 1 sc, sc in next 3 sc, 5 sc in next 4-ch, (2 sc, a p and 1 sc) in each of next three 2-ch spaces, 5 sc in 4-ch. Repeat from * around, making each corner like 1st one. Give Doily a final pressing.

No. 24—ROUND DINNER TABLE DOILY SIZE—14½ inches.

MATERIALS—Lily SIX CORD Mercerized Crochet Cotton. size 30.

Ch 8, sc in 5th st from hook for a p, ch 7, p, ch 3, dtr in starting st, (ch 7, p, ch 7, p, ch 3, dtr in side-top of last dtr) 53 times (54 p-loops). Sl st in starting st—completing circle. **ROW 2**—Sl st to center of 1st p-loop, * (ch 7, p, ch 7, p, ch 3, sc in next p-loop) 8 times, ch 11, sc in next loop. Repeat from * 5 times. **ROW 3**—Sl st to center of 1st p-loop, * (ch 7, p, ch 8, p, ch 3, sc in next loop) 7 times, ch 3, tr in 3d st of next 11-ch, (ch 1, tr in next st) 6 times, ch 3, sc in next p-loop. Repeat from * around. **ROW 4**—Sl st to center of 1st p-loop, * (ch 7, p, ch 8, p, ch 3, sc in next loop) 6 times, ch 7, p, ch 8, p, ch 3, 2 sc between 1st 2 tr of shell, 2 hdc in next 1-ch, 3 dc in next, 1 dc in next tr, 3 dc in next 1-ch, 2 hdc in next, 2 sc in next, ch 7, p, ch 8, p, ch 3, sc in next p-loop. Repeat from * around. **ROW 5**—Sl st to center of 1st p-loop, (ch 8, p, ch 8, p, ch 4, sc in next loop) 6 times, * another p-loop, sc in center dc of next shell, (a p-loop, sc in next p-loop) 8 times. Repeat from * around. **ROW 6**—Sl st to center of 1st p-loop, (ch 8, p, ch 8, p, ch 4, sc in next loop) 6 times, * ch 13, sc in next loop, (ch 8, p, ch 8, p, ch 4, sc in next loop) 8 times. Repeat from * around. **ROW 7**—Sl st to center of 1st loop, (ch 8, p, ch 9, p, ch 4, sc in next loop) 5 times, * ch 3, tr in 3d st of next 13-ch, (ch 1, tr in next st) 8 times, ch 3, sc in next p-loop, (ch 8, p, ch 9, p, ch 4, sc in next loop) 7 times. Repeat from * around. **ROW 8**—Sl st to center of 1st loop, (ch 8, p, ch 9, p, ch 4, sc in next loop) 4 times, * another p-loop, 2 sc between 1st 2 tr of shell, 2 hdc in next 1-ch space, 2 dc in next, 3 dc in next, 1 dc in next tr. 3 dc in next 1-ch. 2 dc in next, 2 hdc in next, 2 sc in next, ** (ch 8, p, ch 9, p, ch 4, sc in next p-loop) 7 times. Repeat from * around. **ROW 9**—Sl st to center of 1st loop, (ch 9, p, ch 9, p, ch 5, sc in next loop) 4 times, * another p-loop, sc in center dc of shell, (a p-loop, sc in next p-loop) 8 times. Repeat from * around. **ROW 10**—Sl st to center of 1st loop, (ch 9, p, ch 9, p, ch 5, sc in next loop) 4 times, * ch 15, sc in next loop, (ch 9, p, ch 9, p, ch 5, sc in next loop) 8 times. Repeat from * around. **ROW 11**—Sl st to center of 1st loop, (ch 9, p, ch 10, p, ch 5, sc in next loop) 3 times, * ch 4, tr in 4th st of next loop, (ch 1, tr in next) 8 times, ch 4, sc in next p-loop, (ch 9, p, ch 10, p, ch 5, sc in next loop) 7 times. Repeat from * around. **ROW 12**—Sl st to center of 1st loop, (ch 9, p, ch 10, p, ch 5, sc in next loop) twice. * Repeat from * to ** in Row 8. (Ch 9, p, ch 10, p, ch 5, sc in next loop) 7 times. Repeat from * around. **ROW 13** —Sl st to center of 1st loop, (ch 10, p, ch 10, p, ch 6, sc in next loop) twice, * another p-loop, sc in center dc of shell, (a p-loop, sc in next loop) 8 times. Repeat from * around. **ROW 14**—Sl st to center of 1st loop, * (ch 7, p, ch 6, p) twice, (ch 6, p) twice, ch 1, sk last 4 ps, 3 tr in next ch st. holding last loop of each tr on hook, thread over and pull thru all 4 loops on hook at once (a Cluster), ch 5, p, ch 6, p, ch 3, sc in next p-loop. * Repeat from * to * once. ** Ch 7, p, (ch 6, p) twice, ch 3, sc in next loop. Repeat from * to * 8 times. Repeat from ** around. Fasten off.

On tissue paper, draw a true circle larger than Doily. Stretch and pin Doily right-side-down on this pattern on ironing board and steam with a wet cloth and hot iron, then press thru a dry cloth until perfectly dry. Cut and hem a circle of linen to go in center and whip to lace.

FLOWER—Wind thread 16 times around the ends of 2 crochet hooks held together, slip off and cover ring with 20 sc. Sl st in 1st sc. **ROW** 2—Ch 4, dc in next sc, (ch l, dc in next sc) 18 times, ch 1, sl st in 3d st of 1st 4-ch. **ROW** 3—(2 sc over next l-ch) 20 times. Sl st in front loop of 1st sc. **ROW** 4—Turn. (ch 5, sc in a single loop of next sc) repeated around. **ROW** 5—Ch 1, turn, sc in remaining back loop of each sc in Row 3. Sl st in front loop of 1st sc. **ROW 6**—Repeat Row 4. **ROW 7**—Ch 1, turn, (1 sc in remaining back loop of next sc of Row 5, 2 sc in back loop of next sc) repeated around. S1 st in back loop of 1st sc. **ROW 8**—* (Work in back loops only of sc). Ch 14, sk last 2 sts, sc in remaining 12 sts, sl st in next sc on center. Ch I, turn, sc in last 10 sc. Ch 2, turn, sc in 10 sc, sl st in next sc on center. Ch I, turn, 8 sc, ch 2, turn, 8 sc, sl st in next sc on center. Ch 1, turn, 6 sc, ch 2, turn, 6 sc, sl st in next sc on center. Ch 1, turn, 4 sc, ch 2, turn, 4 sc, sl st in next sc on center. Ch 1, turn, 2 sc, ch 2, turn, 2 sc, sl st in next 4 sc on center. Repeat from * 5 times. S1 st in each sc midway to 1st petal. Ch 20, sk last st, 1 sc in next one. Then make 25 sc over bal. of ch, sl st in next sc on center. Ch 1, turn, sc in each sc to 2d from end, sl st in end sc. Ch 2, turn, sk sl st and I sc, sc in each sc to center, sl st in next sc on center. Fasten off. Make 6 Flowers. Sew a Flower in center of each section between shells. Give Doily a final pressing.

No. 25—EDGING

WIDTH—¾ inch.

MATERIALS—Lily **SIX CORD** Mercerized Crochet Cotton, size 30.

Make a chain 1½ times desired length. Sk last st, sc in next 2 sts, (ch 6, sk 6 sts of long chain, sc in next 3 sts) repeated to end, making only I sc after final 6-ch. **ROW 2**—Ch I, (9 sc over next 6-ch loop, sl st in 2d of 3 sc between loops) repeated to end. **ROW 3**—Ch 1 and working along opposite side of 1st Row, make * (3 sc, ch 5, sl st in last sc for a p, 3 sc, a p and 3 sc) over next loop, sl st in center st between loops. Repeat from * to end. **ROW 4**—Ch 9, sk 1st 3 sc of Row 2, tr in next sc, * (ch l, tr in next sc) twice, ch 2, tr in 4th sc on next loop. Repeat from * to end. Ch 9, sl st down into end of lace. Fasten off.

No. 26—EDGING

WIDTH—1 inch.

MATERIALS—Lily SIX CORD Mercerized Crochet Cotton, size 30.

Make a chain slightly longer than desired length, dc in 7th st from hook, (ch 1, dc in next 2d st) repeated to end. **ROW 2**—Ch l, turn, (2 sc in next 1-ch space) 3 times, * (1 sc, ch 5, sl st in last sc for a p, and 1 sc) in next 1-ch, 2 sc in next, 1 sc in next, ch 11, turn, sl st in 4th sc to left of p, ch 1, turn, 13 sc over 11-ch, sc in same space on beading, 2 sc in next, ch 8, turn, dc in 7th (center) sc on loop, ch 5, dc in same st, ch 8, sl st in next 3d sc on beading, ch 1, turn, (4 sc, a p, 3 sc, a p and 3 sc) over 8-ch, 3 sc over next 5-ch, (ch 6, sl st in 6th st from hook) 3 times, 3 sc over bal. of same 5-ch, (3 sc, a p, 3 sc, a p and 4 sc) over next 8-ch, (2 sc in next space on beading) 6 times. Repeat from * to end. Fasten off.

No. 27—EDGING

WIDTH—2¼ inches.

MATERIALS—Lily **SIX CORD** Mercerized Crochet Cotton, size 30.

MEDALLION—Wind thread 15 times around ends of 2 crochet hooks held together. Slip off and cover ring with 18 sc, sl st in 1st sc. **ROW 2**—Ch 6, 2 tr in same st, ch 5, sl st in last tr for a p, 3 tr in same sc on center, * ch 6, sl st in 5th st from hook for a p, ch 2, (3 tr, a p and 3 tr) in next 3d sc. Repeat from * 4 times. Ch 6, p, ch 2, sl st in 1st 6-ch. Fasten off. **ROW 3**—Join to one p-loop between shells, (ch 15, sc in next p-loop) 6 times. **ROW 4**—Over each 15-ch loop make 5 sc, a p, (2 sc, a p) 4 times, and 5 sc. Sl st in 1st sc. Fasten off. Tack Medallions together by the 4th and 5th ps on one loop and the 1st and 2d ps on next loop, to corresponding ps on another Medallion. **Heading Row**—Join to 5th p on top, right-hand loop of end Medallion, ch 7 for a dtr, * ch 12, sc in middle p on next loop (center-top), ch 12. dtr in 1st p on next loop, ch 9. dtr in 5th p on next loop on next Medallion. Repeat from * across. **ROW 2**—Ch 1. turn, sc in last dtr, (ch 4, sc over next chain) 4 times across 12-ch, ch 4, sc in next sc. Continue across top of lace in same way, spacing 4-ch loops evenly apart. **ROW 3**—Ch 4, turn, hdc in last loop, (ch 2. hdc in next loop) repeated across. Fasten off.

No. 28—EDGING

WIDTH-⅞ inch.

MATERIALS—Lily SIX CORD Mercerized Crochet Cotton. size 30.

Ch 10, sc in 5th st from hook for a p, (ch 13, p) repeated for desired length. **ROW 2**—Ch 11, turn. 2 tr in 6th at from hook, holding the last loop of each tr on hook, thread over and pull thru all 3 loops on hook at once (a Cluster), (ch 9, a 3-tr-Cluater in center st between next 2 ps) repeated to end. **ROW 3**—Ch I, turn, * (5 sc, ch 5, sl st in last sc for a p, and 5 sc) over next 9-ch, 5 sc over half of next, ch 7, sl st in 6th st from hook, (ch 6, sl st in 6th st from hook) 6 times, sk these 7 ps, sl st in next 1-ch, 5 sc over bal. of 9-ch. Repeat from * to end. Fasten off.

No. 29—EDGING

WIDTH—2 inches.

MATERIALS—Lily **SIX CORD** Mercerized Crochet Cotton, size 30.

Ch 27, ** 2 dc in 5th st from hook, holding last loop of each dc on hook, thread over and pull thru all 3 loops on hook at once (a Cluster), ch 5, sl st in Cluster for a p, ch 4, sl st at base of Cluster. Ch 7, turn, tr in p at tip of Cluster, (ch 2, tr in same p) 6 times, ch 7, sl st at base of Cluster. Ch 1, turn, (1 hdc, 3 dc, 1 hdc and 1 sc) twice over 7-ch, * l hdc and 2 dc in next 2-ch, dc in tr, (2 dc, 1 hdc and l sc) in next 2-ch. Repeat from * twice. (l hdc. 3 dc, 1 hdc and 1 sc) twice over next 7-ch, sl st at base of Cluster, ch 3, sl st in next 4th ch st. Ch 41 and repeat from ** for desired length. After final motif, ch 23, dc in 9th st from hook, (ch 2, dc in next 3d st) repeated across top of lace. In place of final 2-ch and dc, make 5-ch and a sl st. **ROW 2**—Ch 1, 2 sc in next 2-ch space, ch 7, sc in 5th st from hook for a p. ch 12, p, ch 3, sl st in last sc, * 1 sc in bal. of same beading space, 3 sc in next space, 2 sc in next, ch 7, p, ch 3, sc in center of 2d scallop on motif, (ch 7, p) twice, ch 3. sc in center of next scallop, (ch 7, p) twice, ch 3, sc in 2d dc on next scallop, a p-loop, sc in next 2d dc, (a p-loop, sc in center of next scallop) twice, ch 7, p, ch 3, 2 sc in 4th beading space between motifs, 3 sc in next space, 2 sc in next, ch 7, p, ch 12, p, ch 3, sl st in last sc. Repeat from * to end of row. Fasten off. **ROW 3**—Join to 1st p-loop of last row, * ch 6, p, ch 2, sc in next 2-p-loop, (ch 8, p, ch 8, p, ch 4, sc in next p-loop) 4 times, ch 6, p, ch 2, sc in next 2-p-loop. Repeat from * to end. **ROW 4**—Ch 13, turn, sc in next p-loop, * (ch 15, sc in next p-loop) 3 times, ch 5, sc across in next 2-p-loop. Repeat from * to end. Make final loop of 13-ch. **ROW 5**—Ch 1, turn. (8 sc, a 5-ch p and 8 sc) over 13-ch. (9 sc, a p and 9 sc) over each 15-ch loop, 4 sc over 5-ch between scallops.

No. 30—EDGING

WIDTH—1¼ inches.

MATERIALS—Lily **SIX CORD** Mercerized Crochet Cotton, size 30.

Ch 8, sc in 5th st from hook for a p, ch 7, p, ch 3, tr in starting st, (ch 7, p) 3 times, ch 3, turn, sc between ps of 1st p-loop, * (ch 7, p) 3 times, ch 3, turn, sc between last 2 ps of last p-loop. Repeat from * for slightly more than desired length. Ch 9, dc between next 2 ps, (ch 8, dc in next p-loop down side of lace) repeated to end, ch 4, dtr down in end tr. Fasten off. Join to starting st on opposite side, ch 3 for a dc, (ch 9, dc in next p-loop) repeated to end. Fasten off. Join to 3d st of 1st 12-ch, ch 3, (4 dc, ch 5, sl st in last dc for a p, and 4 dc) in next 5th ch st, * ch I, (4 dc, a p and 4 dc) in 5th st of next 9-ch. Repeat from * to end. Ch 3, sl st in end dc. Fasten off.

No. 31—INSERTION

WIDTH—1½ inches.

MATERIALS—Lily SIX CORD Mercerized Crochet Cotton, size 30.

Ch 8, (7 dc, 1 hdc and 1 sc) in 4th st from hook, 3 sc over next 3-ch, 1 sc in next (end) st. * Ch 12, (7 dc, 1 hdc and I sc) in 4th st from hook, 3 sc over next 3 ch sts. Repeat from *for desired length. ** Ch 7, (7 dc. 1 hdc and 1 ac) in 4th st from hook, 3 sc over remaining 3 ch sts, 5 sc over 5-ch between next 2 scallops. Repeat from ** to end. Fasten off.

Edge—Join to 5th dc on 1st scallop, * ch 2, dc in 5th dc on next scallop, (ch 5, sc in 5th st from hook for a p, ch 1, dc in same st) 3 times, ch 2, sc in 5th dc on next scallop. Repeat from * to end. Fasten off. Repeat this same edge on opposite side, making shells exactly opposite those just made.

No. 32—EDGING

WIDTH—1⅝ inches.

MATERIALS—Lily **SIX CORD** Mercerized Crochet Cotton, size 30.

Ch 8, sk last 3 sts, 1 dc in each remaining st. * Ch 6, turn, sk last 4 dc, dc in next dc, ch 3, turn, dc in dc, 4 dc over ⅔'s of next 6-ch. Repeat from * for desired length, making a number of bars to divide evenly by 3, plus 1 bar extra. Fasten off. **ROW 2**—Return to start of row and join to 3-ch loop at top of 1st bar, ch 6, dc in same place, * ch 2, sc in space between bars, ch 2, dc in 3-ch at end of next bar, ch 3, dc in same place. Repeat from * to end. Fasten off. **ROW 3**—Join to 1st 6-ch of last row, ch 10 sc in 5th st from hook for a p, ch 1, tr in same 6-ch, ch 5, p, ch 1, tr in same 6-ch., * ch 4, sc in center of next shell, ch 15, p, ch 8, sk last p, sl st in next 8th ch st, ch 3, sc in next shell, ch 4, tr in center of next shell, (ch 5, p, ch I, tr in same place) 3 times. Repeat from * to end. Fasten off. **ROW 4**—Join to 1st p of last row * ch 2, dtr in p at top of next long loop, (ch 5, p, ch 1, dtr in same place) 7 times, ch 2, sc in center p of next shell. Repeat from * to end. Fasten off.

Simple Crochet Stitches

No. 1—Chain Stitch (CH) Form a loop on thread insert hook on loop and pull thread through tightening threads. Thread over hook and pull through last chain made. Continue chains for length desired.

No. 2—Slip Stitch (SL ST) Make a chain the desired length. Skip one chain, * insert hook in next chain, thread over hook and pull through stitch and loop on hook. Repeat from *. This stitch is used in joining and whenever an invisible stitch is required.

No. 3—Single Crochet (S C) Chain for desired length. skip 1 ch, * insert hook in next ch, thread over hook and pull through ch. There are now 2 loops on hook, thread over hook and pull through both loops, repeat from *. For succeeding rows of s c, ch 1, turn insert hook in top of next st taking up both threads and continue same as first row.

No. 4—Short Double Crochet (S D C) Ch for desired length thread over hook, insert hook in 3rd st from hook, draw thread through (3 loops on hook), thread over and draw through all three loops on hook. For succeeding rows, ch 2, turn.

No. 5—Double Crochet (D C) Ch for desired length, thread over hook, insert hook in 4th st from hook, draw thread through (3 loops on hook) thread over hook and pull through 2 loops thread over hook and pull through 2 loops. Succeeding rows, ch 3, turn and work next d c in 2nd d c of previous row. The ch 3 counts as 1 d c.

No. 6—Treble Crochet (TR C) Ch for desired length, thread over hook twice insert hook in 5th ch from hook draw thread through (4 loops on hook) thread over hook pull through 2 loops thread over, pull through 2 loops, thread over, pull through 2 loops. For succeeding rows ch 4, turn and work next tr c in 2nd tr c of previous row. The ch 4 counts as 1 tr c.

No. 7—Double Treble Crochet (D TR C) Ch for desired length thread over hook 3 times insert in 6th ch from hook (5 loops on hook) and work off 2 loops at a time same as tr c. For succeeding rows ch 5 turn and work next d tr c in 2nd d tr c of previous row. The ch 5 counts as 1 d tr c.

No. 8—Rib Stitch. Work this same as single crochet but insert hook in back loop of stitch only. This is sometimes called the slipper stitch.

No. 9—Picot (P) There are two methods of working the picot. (A) Work a single crochet in the foundation, ch 3 or 4 sts depending on the length of picot desired, sl st in top of s c made. (B) Work an s c, ch 3 or 4 for picot and s c in same space. Work as many single crochets between picots as desired.

No. 10—Open or Filet Mesh (0 M.) When worked on a chain work the first d c in 8th ch from hook * ch 2, skip 2 sts, 1 d c in next st, repeat from *. Succeeding rows ch 5 to turn, d c in d c, ch 2, d c in next d c, repeat from *.

No. 11—Block or Solid Mesh (S M) Four double crochets form 1 solid mesh and 3 d c are required for each additional solid mesh. Open mesh and solid mesh are used in Filet Crochet.

No. 12—Slanting Shell St. Ch for desired length, work 2 d c in 4th st from hook, skip 3 sts, sl st in next st, * ch 3, 2 d c in same st with sl st, skip 3 sts, sl st in next st. Repeat from *. **2nd Row**. Ch 3, turn 2 d c in sl st, sl st in 3 ch loop of shell in previous row, * ch 3, 2 d c in same space, sl st in next shell, repeat from *.

No. 13—Bean or Pop Corn Stitch. Work 3 d c in same space, drop loop from hook insert hook in first d c made and draw loop through, ch 1 to tighten st.

No. 14—Cross Treble Crochet. Ch for desired length, thread over twice, insert in 5th st from hook, * work off two loops, thread over, skip 2 sts, insert in next st and work off all loops on needle 2 at a time, ch 2, d c in center to complete cross. Thread over twice, insert in next st and repeat from *.

No. 15—Cluster Stitch. Work 3 or 4 tr c in same st always retaining the last loop of each tr c on needle, thread over and pull through all loops on needle.

No. 16—Lacet St. Ch for desired length, work 1 s c in 10th st from hook, ch 3 skip 2 sts, 1 d c in next st, * ch 3, skip 2 sts, 1 s c in next st, ch 3, skip 2 sts 1 d c in next st, repeat from * to end of row, 2nd row, d c in d c, ch 5 d c in next d c.

No. 17—Knot Stitch (Sometimes Called Lovers Knot St.) Ch for desired length, * draw a ¼ inch loop on hook, thread over and pull through ch, s c in single loop of st, draw another ¼ inch loop, s c into loop, skip 4 sts, s c in next st, repeat from *. To turn make %" knots, * s c in loop at right of s c and s c in loop at left of s c of previous row, 2 knot sts and repeat from *.

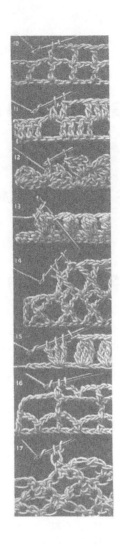

Metric Conversion Chart

CONVERTING INCHES TO CENTIMETERS AND YARDS TO METERS

mm—millimeters cm—centimeters m—meters

INCHES INTO MILLIMETERS AND CENTIMETERS
(Slightly rounded off for convenience)

inches	mm		cm	inches	cm	inches	cm	inches	cm
⅛	3mm			5	12.5	21	53.5	38	96.5
¼	6mm			5½	14	22	56	39	99
⅜	10mm	or	1cm	6	15	23	58.5	40	101.5
½	13mm	or	1.3cm	7	18	24	61	41	104
⅝	15mm	or	1.5cm	8	20.5	25	63.5	42	106.5
¾	20mm	or	2cm	9	23	26	66	43	109
⅞	22mm	or	2.2cm	10	25.5	27	68.5	44	112
1	25mm	or	2.5cm	11	28	28	71	45	114.5
1¼	32mm	or	3.2cm	12	30.5	29	73.5	46	117
1½	38mm	or	3.8cm	13	33	30	76	47	119.5
1¾	45mm	or	4.5cm	14	35.5	31	79	48	122
2	50mm	or	5cm	15	38	32	81.5	49	124.5
2½	65mm	or	6.5cm	16	40.5	33	84	50	127
3	75mm	or	7.5cm	17	43	34	86.5		
3½	90mm	or	9cm	18	46	35	89		
4	100mm	or	10cm	19	48.5	36	91.5		
4½	115mm	or	11.5cm	20	51	37	94		

YARDS TO METERS
(Slightly rounded off for convenience)

yards	meters	yards	meters	yards	meters	yards	meters	yards	meters
1/8	0.15	2 1/8	1.95	4 1/8	3.80	6 1/8	5.60	8 1/8	7.45
1/4	0.25	2 1/4	2.10	4 1/4	3.90	6 1/4	5.75	8 1/4	7.55
3/8	0.35	2 3/8	2.20	4 3/8	4.00	6 3/8	5.85	8 3/8	7.70
1/2	0.50	2 1/2	2.30	4 1/2	4.15	6 1/2	5.95	8 1/2	7.80
5/8	0.60	2 5/8	2.40	4 5/8	4.25	6 5/8	6.10	8 5/8	7.90
3/4	0.70	2 3/4	2.55	4 3/4	4.35	6 3/4	6.20	8 3/4	8.00
7/8	0.80	2 7/8	2.65	4 7/8	4.50	6 7/8	6.30	8 7/8	8.15
1	0.95	3	2.75	5	4.60	7	6.40	9	8.25
1 1/8	1.05	3 1/8	2.90	5 1/8	4.70	7 1/8	6.55	9 1/8	8.35
1 1/4	1.15	3 1/4	3.00	5 1/4	4.80	7 1/4	6.65	9 1/4	8.50
1 3/8	1.30	3 3/8	3.10	5 3/8	4.95	7 3/8	6.75	9 3/8	8.60
1 1/2	1.40	3 1/2	3.20	5 1/2	5.05	7 1/2	6.90	9 1/2	8.70
1 5/8	1.50	3 5/8	3.35	5 5/8	5.15	7 5/8	7.00	9 5/8	8.80
1 3/4	1.60	3 3/4	3.45	5 3/4	5.30	7 3/4	7.10	9 3/4	8.95
1 7/8	1.75	3 7/8	3.55	5 7/8	5.40	7 7/8	7.20	9 7/8	9.05
2	1.85	4	3.70	6	5.50	8	7.35	10	9.15

AVAILABLE FABRIC WIDTHS

25"	65cm	50"	127cm
27"	70cm	54"/56"	140cm
35"/36"	90cm	58"/60"	150cm
39"	100cm	68"/70"	175cm
44"/45"	115cm	72"	180cm
48"	122cm		

AVAILABLE ZIPPER LENGTHS

4"	10cm	10"	25cm
5"	12cm	12"	30cm
6"	15cm	14"	35cm
7"	18cm	16"	40cm
8"	20cm	18"	45cm
9"	22cm	20"	50cm
22"	55cm		
24"	60cm		
26"	65cm		
28"	70cm		
30"	75cm		

Made in the USA
Las Vegas, NV
11 November 2024

11583547R00077